MARXISM

and the

NATIONAL QUESTION

From J. V. Stalin, *Works*, Vol. 2, pp. 300-81
Foreign Languages Publishing House,
Moscow, 1954

Reprinted by Red Star Publishers, 2015
www.RedStarPublishers.org

CONTENTS

MARXISM AND THE NATIONAL QUESTION

I.	The Nation	7
II.	The National Movement	14
III.	Presentation of the Question	21
IV.	Cultural-National Autonomy	27
V.	The Bund, Its Nationalism, Its Separatism	36
VI.	The Caucasians, the Conference of the Liquidators	47
VII.	The National Question in Russia	56
Notes		63

MARXISM AND THE NATIONAL QUESTION[1]

The period of counter-revolution in Russia brought not only "thunder and lightning" in its train, but also disillusionment in the movement and lack of faith in common forces. As long as people believed in "a bright future," they fought side by side irrespective of nationality – common questions first and foremost! But when doubt crept into people's hearts, they began to depart, each to his own national tent – let every man count only upon himself! The "national question" first and foremost!

At the same time a profound upheaval was taking place in the economic life of the country. The year 1905 had not been in vain: one more blow had been struck at the survivals of serfdom in the countryside. The series of good harvests which succeeded the famine years, and the industrial boom which followed, furthered the progress of capitalism. Class differentiation in the countryside, the growth of the towns, the development of trade and means of communication all took a big stride forward. This applied particularly to the border regions. And it could not but hasten the process of economic consolidation of the nationalities of Russia. They were bound to be stirred into movement....

The "constitutional regime" established at that time also acted in the same direction of awakening the nationalities. The spread of newspapers and of literature generally, a certain freedom of the press and cultural institutions, an increase in the number of national theatres, and so forth, all unquestionably helped to strengthen "national sentiments." The Duma, with its election campaign and political groups, gave fresh opportunities for greater activity of the nations and provided a new and wide arena for their mobilisation.

And the mounting wave of militant nationalism above and the series of repressive measures taken by the "powers that be" in vengeance on the border regions for their "love of freedom," evoked an answering wave of nationalism below, which at times took the form of crude chauvinism. The spread of Zionism[2] among the Jews, the increase of chauvinism in Poland, Pan-Islamism among the Tatars, the spread of nationalism among the Armenians, Georgians and Ukrainians, the general swing of the philistine towards anti-Semitism – all these are generally known facts.

The wave of nationalism swept onwards with increasing force, threatening to engulf the mass of the workers. And the more the movement for emancipation declined, the more plentifully nationalism pushed forth its blossoms.

At this difficult time Social-Democracy had a high mission – to resist nationalism and to protect the masses from the general "epidemic." For Social-Democracy, and Social-Democracy alone, could do this, by countering nationalism with the tried weapon of internationalism, with the unity and indivisibility of the class struggle. And the more powerfully the wave of nationalism advanced, the louder had to be the call of Social-Democracy for fraternity and unity among the proletarians of all the nationalities of Russia. And in this connection particular firmness was demanded of the Social-Democrats of the border regions, who came into direct contact with the nationalist movement.

But not all Social-Democrats proved equal to the task – and this applies particularly to the Social-Democrats of the border regions. The Bund, which had previously laid stress on the common tasks, now began to give prominence to its own specific, purely nationalist aims: it went to the length of declaring "observance of the Sabbath" and "recognition of Yiddish" a fighting issue in its election campaign.* The Bund was followed by the Caucasus; one section of the Caucasian Social-Democrats, which, like the rest of the Caucasian Social-Democrats, had formerly rejected "cultural-national autonomy," are now making it an immediate demand.† This is without mentioning the conference of the Liquidators, which in a diplomatic way gave its sanction to nationalist vacillations.‡

But from this it follows that the views of Russian Social-Democracy on the national question are not yet clear to all Social-Democrats.

It is evident that a serious and comprehensive discussion of the national question is required. Consistent Social-Democrats must work solidly and indefatigably against the fog of nationalism, no matter from what quarter it proceeds.

---

* See "Report of the Ninth Conference of the Bund."

† See "Announcement of the August Conference."

‡ *Ibid.*

I

THE NATION

What is a nation?

A nation is primarily a community, a definite community of people.

This community is not racial, nor is it tribal. The modern Italian nation was formed from Romans, Teutons, Etruscans, Greeks, Arabs, and so forth. The French nation was formed from Gauls, Romans, Britons, Teutons, and so on. The same must be said of the British, the Germans and others, who were formed into nations from people of diverse races and tribes.

Thus, a nation is not a racial or tribal, but a historically constituted community of people.

On the other hand, it is unquestionable that the great empires of Cyrus and Alexander could not be called nations, although they came to be constituted historically and were formed out of different tribes and races. They were not nations, but casual and loosely-connected conglomerations of groups, which fell apart or joined together according to the victories or defeats of this or that conqueror.

Thus, a nation is not a casual or ephemeral conglomeration, but a stable community of people.

But not every stable community constitutes a nation. Austria and Russia are also stable communities, but nobody calls them nations. What distinguishes a national community from a state community? The fact, among others, that a national community is inconceivable without a common language, while a state need not have a common language. The Czech nation in Austria and the Polish in Russia would be impossible if each did not have a common language, whereas the integrity of Russia and Austria is not affected by the fact that there are a number of different languages within their borders. We are referring, of course, to the spoken languages of the people and not to the official governmental languages.

Thus, *a common language* is one of the characteristic features of a nation.

This, of course, does not mean that different nations always and everywhere speak different languages, or that all who speak one language necessarily constitute one nation. A *common* language for every nation, but not necessarily different languages for different nations! There is no nation which at one and the same time speaks several languages, but this does not mean that there cannot be two nations speaking the same language! Englishmen and Americans speak one language, but they do not constitute one nation. The same is true of the Norwegians and the Danes, the English and the Irish.

But why, for instance, do the English and the Americans not constitute one nation in spite of their common language?

Firstly, because they do not live together, but inhabit different territories. A nation is formed only as a result of lengthy and systematic intercourse, as a result of people living together generation after generation.

But people cannot live together for lengthy periods unless they have a common territory. Englishmen and Americans originally inhabited the same territory, England, and constituted one nation. Later, one section of the English emigrated from England to a new territory, America, and there, in the new territory, in the course of time, came to form the new American nation. Difference of territory led to the formation of different nations.

Thus, *a common territory* is one of the characteristic features of a nation.

But this is not all. Common territory does not by itself create a nation. This requires, in addition, an internal economic bond to weld the various parts of the nation into a single whole. There is no such bond between England and America, and so they constitute two different nations. But the Americans themselves would not deserve to be called a nation were not the different parts of America bound together into an economic whole, as a result of division of labour between them, the development of means of communication, and so forth.

Take the Georgians, for instance. The Georgians before the Reform inhabited a common territory and spoke one language. Nevertheless, they did not, strictly speaking, constitute one nation, for, being split up into a number of disconnected principalities, they could not share a common economic life; for centuries they waged war against each other and pillaged each other, each inciting the Persians and Turks against the other. The ephemeral and casual union of the principalities which some successful king sometimes managed to bring about embraced at best a superficial administrative sphere, and rapidly disintegrated owing to the caprices of the princes and the indifference of the peasants. Nor could it be otherwise in economically disunited Georgia.... Georgia came on the scene as a nation only in the latter half of the nineteenth century, when the fall of serfdom and the growth of the economic life of the country, the development of means of communication and the rise of capitalism, introduced division of labour between the various districts of Georgia, completely shattered the economic isolation of the principalities and bound them together into a single whole.

The same must be said of the other nations which have passed through the stage of feudalism and have developed capitalism.

Thus, *a common economic life, economic cohesion*, is one of the characteristic features of a nation.

But even this is not all. Apart from the foregoing, one must take into consideration the specific spiritual complexion of the people constituting a nation. Nations differ not only in their conditions of life, but also in spiritual complexion, which manifests itself in peculiarities of national culture. If England, America and Ireland, which speak one language, nevertheless constitute three distinct nations, it is in no small measure due to the peculiar psychological make-up which they developed from generation to generation as a result of dissimilar conditions of existence.

Of course, by itself, psychological make-up or, as it is otherwise called, "national character," is something intangible for the observer, but in so far as it manifests itself in a distinctive culture common to the nation it is something tangible and cannot be ignored.

Needless to say, "national character" is not a thing that is fixed once and for all, but is modified by changes in the conditions of life; but since it exists at every given moment, it leaves its impress on the physiognomy of the nation.

Thus, *a common psychological make-up*, which manifests itself in a common culture, is one of the characteristic features of a nation.

We have now exhausted the characteristic features of a nation.

A nation is a historically constituted, stable community of people, formed on the basis of a common language, territory, economic life, and psychological make-up manifested in a common culture.

It goes without saying that a nation, like every historical phenomenon, is subject to the law of change, has its history, its beginning and end.

It must be emphasised that none of the above characteristics taken separately is sufficient to define a nation. More than that, it is sufficient for a single one of these characteristics to be lacking and the nation ceases to be a nation.

It is possible to conceive of people possessing a common "national character" who, nevertheless, cannot be said to constitute a single nation if they are economically disunited, inhabit different territories, speak different languages, and so forth. Such, for instance, are the Russian, Galician, American, Georgian and Caucasian Highland *Jews*, who, in our opinion, do not constitute a single nation.

It is possible to conceive of people with a common territory and economic life who nevertheless would not constitute a single nation because they have no common language and no common "national character." Such, for instance, are the Germans and Letts in the Baltic region.

Finally, the Norwegians and the Danes speak one language, but they do not constitute a single nation owing to the absence of the other characteristics.

It is only when all these characteristics are present together that we have a nation.

It might appear that "national character" is not one of the characteristics but the sole essential characteristic of a nation, and that all the other characteristics are, properly speaking, only conditions for the development of a nation, rather than its characteristics. Such, for instance, is the view held by R. Springer, and more particularly by O. Bauer, who are Social-Democratic theoreticians on the national question well known in Austria.

Let us examine their theory of the nation,

According to Springer, "a nation is a union of similarly thinking and similarly speaking persons." It is "a cultural community of modern people *no longer tied to the 'soil'*"[*] (our italics).

Thus, a "union" of similarly thinking and similarly speaking people, no matter how disconnected they may be, no matter where they live, is a nation.

Bauer goes even further.

---

[*] See R. Springer, *The National Problem*, Obshchestvennaya Polza Publishing House, 1909, p. 43.

"What is a nation?" he asks. "Is it a common language which makes people a nation? But the English and the Irish... speak the same language without, however, being one people; the Jews have no common language and yet are a nation."[*]

What, then, is a nation?

"A nation is a relative community of character."[†]

But what is character, in this case national character?

National character is "the sum total of characteristics which distinguish the people of one nationality from the people of another nationality – the complex of physical and spiritual characteristics which distinguish one nation from another."[‡]

Bauer knows, of course, that national character does not drop from the skies, and he therefore adds:

"The character of people is determined by nothing so much as by their destiny.... A nation is nothing but a community with a common destiny" which, in turn, is determined "by the conditions under which people produce their means of subsistence and distribute the products of their labour."[§]

We thus arrive at the most "complete," as Bauer calls it, definition of a nation:

"*A nation is an aggregate of people bound into a community of character by a common destiny.*"[**]

We thus have common national character based on a common destiny, but not necessarily connected with a common territory, language or economic life.

But what in that case remains of the nation? What common nationality can there be among people who are economically disconnected, inhabit different territories and from generation to generation speak different languages.

Bauer speaks of the Jews as a nation, although they "have no common language";[††] but what "common destiny" and national

---

[*] See O. Bauer, *The National Question and Social-Democracy*, Serp Publishing House, 1909, pp. 1-2.

[†] *Ibid.*, p. 6.

[‡] *Ibid.*, p. 2.

[§] *Ibid.*, p. 24-25.

[**] *Ibid.*, p. 139.

[††] *Ibid.*, p. 2.

cohesion is there, for instance, between the Georgian, Daghestanian, Russian and American Jews, who are completely separated from one another, inhabit different territories and speak different languages?

The above-mentioned Jews undoubtedly lead their economic and political life in common with the Georgians, Daghestanians, Russians and Americans respectively, and they live in the same cultural atmosphere as these; this is bound to leave a definite impression on their national character; if there is anything common to them left, it is their religion, their common origin and certain relics of the national character. All this is beyond question. But how can it be seriously maintained that petrified religious rites and fading psychological relics affect the "destiny" of these Jews more powerfully than the living social, economic and cultural environment that surrounds them? And it is only on this assumption that it is possible to speak of the Jews as a single nation at all.

What, then, distinguishes Bauer's nation from the mystical and self-sufficient "national spirit" of the spiritualists?

Bauer sets up an impassable barrier between the "distinctive feature" of nations (national character) and the "conditions" of their life, divorcing the one from the other. But what is national character if not a reflection of the conditions of life, a coagulation of impressions derived from environment? How can one limit the matter to national character alone, isolating and divorcing it from the soil that gave rise to it?

Further, what indeed distinguished the English nation from the American nation at the end of the eighteenth and the beginning of the nineteenth centuries, when America was still known as New England? Not national character, of course; for the Americans had originated from England and had brought with them to America not only the English language, but also the English national character, which, of course, they could not lose so soon; although, under the influence of the new conditions, they would naturally be developing their own specific character. Yet, despite their more or less common character, they at that time already constituted a nation distinct from England! Obviously, New England as a nation differed then from England as a nation not by its specific national character, or not so much by its national character, as by its environment and conditions of life, which were distinct from those of England.

It is therefore clear that there is in fact no *single* distinguishing characteristic of a nation. There is only a sum total of characteristics, of which, when nations are compared, sometimes one characteristic (national character), sometimes another (language), or sometimes a third (territory, economic conditions), stands out in sharper relief. A nation constitutes the combination of all these characteristics taken together.

Bauer's point of view, which identifies a nation with its national character, divorces the nation from its soil and converts it into an invisible, self-contained force. The result is not a living and active nation, but something mystical, intangible and supernatural. For, I repeat, what sort of nation, for instance, is a Jewish nation which consists of Georgian, Daghestanian, Russian, American and other Jews, the members of which do not understand each other (since they speak different languages), inhabit different parts of the globe, will never see each other, and will never act together, whether in time of peace or in time of war?!

No, it is not for such paper "nations" that Social-Democracy draws up its national programme. It can reckon only with real nations, which act and move, and therefore insist on being reckoned with.

Bauer is obviously confusing *nation*, which is a historical category, with *tribe*, which is an ethnographical category.

However, Bauer himself apparently feels the weakness of his position. While in the beginning of his book he definitely declares the Jews to be a nation,[*] he corrects himself at the end of the book and states that "in general capitalist society makes it impossible for them (the Jews) to continue as a nation,"[†] by causing them to assimilate with other nations. The reason, it appears, is that "the Jews have no closed territory of settlement,"[‡] whereas the Czechs, for instance, have such a territory and, according to Bauer, will survive as a nation. In short, the reason lies in the absence of a territory.

By arguing thus, Bauer wanted to prove that the Jewish workers cannot demand national autonomy,[§] but he thereby inadvertently

---

[*] See p. 2 of his book.

[†] *Ibid.*, p. 389.

[‡] *Ibid.*, p. 388.

[§] *Ibid.*, p. 396.

refuted his own theory, which denies that a common territory is one of the characteristics of a nation.

But Bauer goes further. In the beginning of his book he definitely declares that "the Jews have no common language, and yet are a nation."[*] But hardly has he reached p. 130 than he effects a change of front and just as definitely declares that "*unquestionably, no nation is possible without a common language*"[†] (our italics).

Bauer wanted to prove that "language is the most important instrument of human intercourse,"[‡] but at the same time he inadvertently proved something he did not mean to prove, namely, the unsoundness of his own theory of nations, which denies the significance of a common language.

Thus this theory, stitched together by idealistic threads, refutes itself.

II

THE NATIONAL MOVEMENT

A nation is not merely a historical category but a historical category belonging to a definite epoch, the epoch of rising capitalism. The process of elimination of feudalism and development of capitalism is at the same time a process of the constitution of people into nations. Such, for instance, was the case in Western Europe. The British, French, Germans, Italians and others were formed into nations at the time of the victorious advance of capitalism and its triumph over feudal disunity.

But the formation of nations in those instances at the same time signified their conversion into independent national states. The British, French and other nations are at the same time British, etc., states. Ireland, which did not participate in this process, does not alter the general picture.

Matters proceeded somewhat differently in Eastern Europe. Whereas in the West nations developed into states, in the East multinational states were formed, states consisting of several nationalities. Such are Austria-Hungary and Russia. In Austria, the Germans proved to be politically the most developed, and they took it upon

---

[*] *Ibid.*, p. 2.

[†] *Ibid.*, p. 130.

[‡] *Ibid.*

themselves to unite the Austrian nationalities into a state. In Hungary, the most adapted for state organisation were the Magyars – the core of the Hungarian nationalities – and it was they who united Hungary. In Russia, the uniting of the nationalities was undertaken by the Great Russians, who were headed by a historically formed, powerful and well-organised aristocratic military bureaucracy.

That was how matters proceeded in the East.

This special method of formation of states could take place only where feudalism had not yet been eliminated, where capitalism was feebly developed, where the nationalities which had been forced into the background had not yet been able to consolidate themselves economically into integral nations.

But capitalism also began to develop in the Eastern states. Trade and means of communication were developing. Large towns were springing up. The nations were becoming economically consolidated. Capitalism, erupting into the tranquil life of the nationalities which had been pushed into the background, was arousing them and stirring them into action. The development of the press and the theatre, the activity of the Reichsrat (Austria) and of the Duma (Russia) were helping to strengthen "national sentiments." The intelligentsia that had arisen was being imbued with "the national idea" and was acting in the same direction....

But the nations which had been pushed into the background and had now awakened to independent life, could no longer form themselves into independent national states; they encountered on their path the very powerful resistance of the ruling strata of the dominant nations, which had long ago assumed the control of the state. They were too late!...

In this way the Czechs, Poles, etc., formed themselves into nations in Austria; the Croats, etc., in Hungary; the Letts, Lithuanians, Ukrainians, Georgians, Armenians, etc., in Russia. What had been an exception in Western Europe (Ireland) became the rule in the East.

In the West, Ireland responded to its exceptional position by a national movement. In the East, the awakened nations were bound to respond in the same fashion.

Thus arose the circumstances which impelled the young nations of Eastern Europe on to the path of struggle.

The struggle began and flared up, to be sure, not between nations as a whole, but between the ruling classes of the dominant nations and of those that had been pushed into the background. The struggle is usually conducted by the urban petty bourgeoisie of the oppressed nation against the big bourgeoisie of the dominant nation (Czechs and Germans), or by the rural bourgeoisie of the oppressed nation against the landlords of the dominant nation (Ukrainians in Poland), or by the whole "national" bourgeoisie of the oppressed nations against the ruling nobility of the dominant nation (Poland, Lithuania and the Ukraine in Russia).

The bourgeoisie plays the leading role.

The chief problem for the young bourgeoisie is the problem of the market. Its aim is to sell its goods and to emerge victorious from competition with the bourgeoisie of a different nationality. Hence its desire to secure its "own," its "home" market. The market is the first school in which the bourgeoisie learns its nationalism.

But matters are usually not confined to the market. The semi-feudal, semi-bourgeois bureaucracy of the dominant nation intervenes in the struggle with its own methods of "arresting and preventing." The bourgeoisie – whether big or small – of the dominant nation is able to deal more "swiftly" and "decisively" with its competitor. "Forces" are united and a series of restrictive measures is put into operation against the "alien" bourgeoisie, measures passing into acts of repression. The struggle spreads from the economic sphere to the political sphere. Restriction of freedom of movement, repression of language, restriction of franchise, closing of schools, religious restrictions, and so on, are piled upon the head of the "competitor." Of course, such measures are designed not only in the interest of the bourgeois classes of the dominant nation, but also in furtherance of the specifically caste aims, so to speak, of the ruling bureaucracy.

But from the point of view of the results achieved this is quite immaterial; the bourgeois classes and the bureaucracy in this matter go hand in hand – whether it be in Austria-Hungary or in Russia.

The bourgeoisie of the oppressed nation, repressed on every hand, is naturally stirred into movement. It appeals to its "native folk" and begins to shout about the "fatherland," claiming that its own cause is the cause of the nation as a whole. It recruits itself an army from among its "countrymen" in the interests of... the "fatherland." Nor do the "folk" always remain unresponsive to its appeals; they rally around its banner: the repression from above affects them too and provokes their discontent.

Thus the national movement begins.

The strength of the national movement is determined by the degree to which the wide strata of the nation, the proletariat and peasantry, participate in it.

Whether the proletariat rallies to the banner of bourgeois nationalism depends on the degree of development of class antagonisms, on the class consciousness and degree of organisation of the proletariat. The class-conscious proletariat has its own tried banner, and has no need to rally to the banner of the bourgeoisie.

As far as the peasants are concerned, their participation in the national movement depends primarily on the character of the repressions. If the repressions affect the "land," as was the case in Ireland, then the mass of the peasants immediately rally to the banner of the national movement.

On the other hand, if, for example, there is no serious *anti-Russian* nationalism in Georgia, it is primarily because there are neither Russian landlords nor a Russian big bourgeoisie there to supply the fuel for such nationalism among the masses. In Georgia there is *anti-Armenian* nationalism; but this is because there is still an Armenian big bourgeoisie there which, by getting the better of the small and still unconsolidated Georgian bourgeoisie, drives the latter to anti-Armenian nationalism.

Depending on these factors, the national movement either assumes a mass character and steadily grows (as in Ireland and Galicia), or is converted into a series of petty collisions, degenerating into squabbles and "fights" over signboards (as in some of the small towns of Bohemia).

The content of the national movement, of course, can not everywhere be the same: it is wholly determined by the diverse demands made by the movement. In Ireland the movement bears an agrarian character; in Bohemia it bears a "language" character; in one place the demand is for civil equality and religious freedom, in another for the nation's "own" officials, or its own Diet. The diversity of demands not infrequently reveals the diverse features which characterise a nation in general (language, territory, etc.). It is worthy of note that we never meet with a demand based on Bauer's all-embracing "national character." And this is natural: "national char-

18

acter" *in itself* is something intangible, and, as was correctly remarked by J. Strasser, "a politician can't do anything with it."*

Such, in general, are the forms and character of the national movement.

From what has been said it will be clear that the national struggle under the conditions of *rising* capitalism is a struggle of the bourgeois classes among themselves. Sometimes the bourgeoisie succeeds in drawing the proletariat into the national movement, and then the national struggle *externally* assumes a "nation-wide" character. But this is so only externally. *In its essence* it is always a bourgeois struggle, one that is to the advantage and profit mainly of the bourgeoisie.

But it does not by any means follow that the proletariat should not put up a fight against the policy of national oppression.

Restriction of freedom of movement, disfranchisement, repression of language, closing of schools, and other forms of persecution affect the workers no less, if not more, than the bourgeoisie. Such a state of affairs can only serve to retard the free development of the intellectual forces of the proletariat of subject nations. One cannot speak seriously of a full development of the intellectual faculties of the Tatar or Jewish worker if he is not allowed to use his native language at meetings and lectures, and if his schools are closed down.

But the policy of nationalist persecution is dangerous to the cause of the proletariat also on another account. It diverts the attention of large strata from social questions, questions of the class struggle, to national questions, questions "common" to the proletariat and the bourgeoisie. And this creates a favourable soil for lying propaganda about "harmony of interests," for glossing over the class interests of the proletariat and for the intellectual enslavement of the workers.

This creates a serious obstacle to the cause of uniting the workers of all nationalities. If a considerable proportion of the Polish workers are still in intellectual bondage to the bourgeois nationalists, if they still stand aloof from the international labour movement, it is chiefly because the age-old anti-Polish policy of the "powers that be" creates the soil for this bondage and hinders the emancipation of the workers from it.

---

* See his *Der Arbeiter und die Nation*, 1912, p. 33.

But the policy of persecution does not stop there. It not infrequently passes from a "system" of *oppression* to a "system" of *inciting* nations against each other, to a "system" of massacres and pogroms. Of course, the latter system is not everywhere and always possible, but where it is possible – in the absence of elementary civil rights – it frequently assumes horrifying proportions and threatens to drown the cause of unity of the workers in blood and tears. The Caucasus and South Russia furnish numerous examples. "Divide and rule" – such is the purpose of the policy of incitement. And where such a policy succeeds, it is a tremendous evil for the proletariat and a serious obstacle to the cause of uniting the workers of all the nationalities in the state.

But the workers are interested in the complete amalgamation of all their fellow-workers into a single international army, in their speedy and final emancipation from intellectual bondage to the bourgeoisie, and in the full and free development of the intellectual forces of their brothers, whatever nation they may belong to.

The workers therefore combat and will continue to combat the policy of national oppression in all its forms, from the most subtle to the most crude, as well as the policy of inciting nations against each other in all its forms.

Social-Democracy in all countries therefore proclaims the right of nations to self-determination.

The right of self-determination means that only the nation itself has the right to determine its destiny, that no one has the right *forcibly* to interfere in the life of the nation, to *destroy* its schools and other institutions, to *violate* its habits and customs, to *repress* its language, or *curtail* its rights.

This, of course, does not mean that Social-Democracy will support every custom and institution of a nation. While combating the coercion of any nation, it will uphold only the right of the *nation* itself to determine its own destiny, at the same time agitating against harmful customs and institutions of that nation in order to enable the toiling strata of the nation to emancipate themselves from them.

The right of self-determination means that a nation may arrange its life in the way it wishes. It has the right to arrange its life on the basis of autonomy. It has the right to enter into federal relations with other nations. It has the right to complete secession. Nations are sovereign, and all nations have equal rights.

This, of course, does not mean that Social-Democracy will support every demand of a nation. A nation has the right even to return to the old order of things; but this does not mean that Social-Democracy will subscribe to such a decision if taken by some institution of a particular nation. The obligations of Social-Democracy, which defends the interests of the proletariat, and the rights of a nation, which consists of various classes, are two different things.

In fighting for the right of nations to self-determination, the aim of Social-Democracy is to put an end to the policy of national oppression, to render it impossible, and thereby to remove the grounds of strife between nations, to take the edge off that strife and reduce it to a minimum.

This is what essentially distinguishes the policy of the class-conscious proletariat from the policy of the bourgeoisie, which attempts to aggravate and fan the national struggle and to prolong and sharpen the national movement.

And that is why the class-conscious proletariat cannot rally under the "national" flag of the bourgeoisie.

That is why the so-called "evolutionary national" policy advocated by Bauer cannot become the policy of the proletariat. Bauer's attempt to identify his "evolutionary national" policy with the policy of the "modern working class"[*] is an attempt to adapt the class struggle of the workers to the struggle of the nations.

The fate of a national movement, which is essentially a bourgeois movement, is naturally bound up with the fate of the bourgeoisie. The final disappearance of a national movement is possible only with the downfall of the bourgeoisie. Only under the reign of socialism can peace be fully established. But even within the framework of capitalism it is possible to reduce the national struggle to a minimum, to undermine it at the root, to render it as harmless as possible to the proletariat. This is borne out, for example, by Switzerland and America. It requires that the country should be democratised and the nations be given the opportunity of free development.

---

[*] See Bauer's book, p. 166.

III

PRESENTATION OF THE QUESTION

A nation has the right freely to determine its own destiny. It has the right to arrange its life as it sees fit, without, of course, trampling on the rights of other nations. That is beyond dispute.

But *how* exactly should it arrange its own life, *what forms* should its future constitution take, if the interests of the majority of the nation and, above all, of the proletariat are to be borne in mind?

A nation has the right to arrange its life on autonomous lines. It even has the right to secede. But this does not mean that it should do so under all circumstances, that autonomy, or separation, will everywhere and always be advantageous for a nation, i.e., for its majority, i.e., for the toiling strata. The Transcaucasian Tatars as a nation may assemble, let us say, in their Diet and, succumbing to the influence of their beys and mullahs, decide to restore the old order of things and to secede from the state. According to the meaning of the clause on self-determination they are fully entitled to do so. But will this be in the interest of the toiling strata of the Tatar nation? Can Social-Democracy look on indifferently when the beys and mullahs assume the leadership of the masses in the solution of the national question?

Should not Social-Democracy interfere in the matter and influence the will of the nation in a definite way? Should it not come forward with a definite plan for the solution of the question, a plan which would be most advantageous for the Tatar masses?

But what solution would be most compatible with the interests of the toiling masses? Autonomy, federation or separation?

All these are problems the solution of which will depend on the concrete historical conditions in which the given nation finds itself.

More than that; conditions, like everything else, change, and a decision which is correct at one particular time may prove to be entirely unsuitable at another.

In the middle of the nineteenth century Marx was in favour of the secession of Russian Poland; and he was right, for it was then a question of emancipating a higher culture from a lower culture that was destroying it. And the question at that time was not only a theoretical one, an academic question, but a practical one, a question of actual reality....

At the end of the nineteenth century the Polish Marxists were already declaring against the secession of Poland; and they too were right, for during the fifty years that had elapsed profound changes had taken place, bringing Russia and Poland closer economically and culturally. Moreover, during that period the question of secession had been converted from a practical matter into a matter of academic dispute, which excited nobody except perhaps intellectuals abroad.

This, of course, by no means precludes the possibility that certain internal and external conditions may arise in which the question of the secession of Poland may again come on the order of the day.

The solution of the national question is possible only in connection with the historical conditions taken in their development.

The economic, political and cultural conditions of a given nation constitute the only key to the question *how* a particular nation ought to arrange its life and *what forms* its future constitution ought to take. It is possible that a specific solution of the question will be required for each nation. If the dialectical approach to a question is required anywhere it is required here, in the national question.

In view of this we must declare our decided opposition to a certain very widespread, but very summary manner of "solving" the national question, which owes its inception to the Bund. We have in mind the easy method of referring to Austrian and South-Slav[*] Social-Democracy, which has supposedly already solved the national question and whose solution the Russian Social-Democrats should simply borrow. It is assumed that whatever, say, is right for Austria is also right for Russia. The most important and decisive factor is lost sight of here, namely, the concrete historical conditions in Russia as a whole and in the life of each of the nations inhabiting Russia in particular.

Listen, for example, to what the well-known Bundist, V. Kossovsky, says:

"When at the Fourth Congress of the Bund the principles of the question (i.e., the national question – *J. St.*) were discussed, the proposal made by one of the members of the congress to settle the

---

[*] South-Slav Social-Democracy operates in the southern part of Austria.

question in the spirit of the resolution of the South-Slav Social-Democratic Party met with general approval."[*]

And the result was that "the congress unanimously adopted"... national autonomy.

And that was all! No analysis of the actual conditions in Russia, no investigation of the condition of the Jews in Russia. They first borrowed the solution of the South-Slav Social-Democratic Party, then they "approved" it, and finally they "unanimously adopted" it! This is the way the Bundists present and "solve" the national question in Russia....

As a matter of fact, Austria and Russia represent entirely different conditions. This explains why the Social-Democrats in Austria, when they adopted their national programme at Brünn (1899)[3] in the spirit of the resolution of the South-Slav Social-Democratic Party (with certain insignificant amendments, it is true), approached the question in an entirely non-Russian way, so to speak, and, of course, solved it in a non-Russian way.

First, as to the presentation of the question. How is the question presented by the Austrian theoreticians of cultural-national autonomy, the interpreters of the Brünn national programme and the resolution of the South-Slav Social-Democratic Party, Springer and Bauer?

"Whether a multi-national state is possible," says Springer, "and whether, in particular, the Austrian nationalities are obliged to form a single political entity, is a question we shall not answer here but shall assume to be settled. For anyone who will not concede this possibility and necessity, our investigation will, of course, be purposeless. Our theme is as follows: inasmuch as these nations are *obliged* to live together, what *legal forms* will enable them *to live together in the best possible way?*" (Springer's italics).[†]

Thus, the starting point is the state integrity of Austria.

Bauer says the same thing:

"We therefore start from the assumption that the Austrian nations will remain in the same state union in which they exist at pre-

---

[*] See V. Kossovsky, *Problems of Nationality*, 1907, pp. 16-17.

[†] See Springer, *The National Problem*, p. 14.

sent and inquire how the nations within this union will arrange their relations among themselves and to the state."*

Here again the first thing is the integrity of Austria.

Can Russian Social-Democracy present the question *in this way*? No, it cannot. And it cannot because from the very outset it holds the view of the right of nations to self-determination, by virtue of which a nation has the right of secession.

Even the Bundist Goldblatt admitted at the Second Congress of Russian Social-Democracy that the latter could not abandon the standpoint of self-determination. Here is what Goldblatt said on that occasion:

"Nothing can be said against the right of self-determination. If any nation is striving for independence, we must not oppose it. If Poland does not wish to enter into 'lawful wedlock' with Russia, it is not for us to interfere with her."

All this is true. But it follows that the starting points of the Austrian and Russian Social-Democrats, far from being identical, are diametrically opposite. After this, can there be any question of borrowing the national programme of the Austrians?

Furthermore, the Austrians hope to achieve the "freedom of nationalities" by means of petty reforms, by slow steps. While they propose cultural-national autonomy as a practical measure, they do not count on any radical change, on a democratic movement for liberation, which they do not even contemplate. The Russian Marxists, on the other hand, associate the "freedom of nationalities" with a probable radical change, with a democratic movement for liberation, having no grounds for counting on reforms. And this essentially alters matters in regard to the probable fate of the nations of Russia.

"Of course," says Bauer, "there is little probability that national autonomy will be the result of a great decision, of a bold action. Austria will develop towards national autonomy step by step, by a slow process of development, in the course of a severe struggle, as a consequence of which legislation and administration will be in a state of chronic paralysis. The new constitution will not be created

---

* See Bauer, *The National Question and Social-Democracy*, p. 399.

by a great legislative act, but by a multitude of separate enactments for individual provinces and individual communities."[*]

Springer says the same thing.

"I am very well aware," he writes, "that institutions of this kind (i.e., organs of national autonomy – *J. St.*) are not created in a single year or a single decade. The reorganisation of the Prussian administration alone took considerable time.... It took the Prussians two decades finally to establish their basic administrative institutions. Let nobody think that I harbour any illusions as to the time required and the difficulties to be overcome in Austria."[†]

All this is very definite. But can the Russian Marxists avoid associating the national question with "bold actions"? Can they count on partial reforms, on "a multitude of separate enactments" as a means for achieving the "freedom of nationalities"? But if they cannot and must not do so, is it not clear that the methods of struggle of the Austrians and the Russians and their prospects must be entirely different? How in such a state of affairs can they confine themselves to the one-sided, milk-and-water cultural-national autonomy of the Austrians? One or the other: either those who are in favour of borrowing do not count on "bold actions" in Russia, or they do count on such actions but "know not what they do."

Finally, the immediate tasks facing Russia and Austria are entirely different and consequently dictate different methods of solving the national question. In Austria parliamentarism prevails, and under present conditions no development in Austria is possible without parliament. But parliamentary life and legislation in Austria are frequently brought to a complete standstill by severe conflicts between the national parties. That explains the chronic political crisis from which Austria has for a long time been suffering. Hence, in Austria the national question is the very hub of political life; it is the vital question. It is therefore not surprising that the Austrian Social-Democratic politicians should first of all try in one way or another to find a solution for the national conflicts – of course on the basis of the existing parliamentary system, by parliamentary methods....

Not so with Russia. In the first place, in Russia "there is no parliament, thank God."[4] In the second place – and this is the main

---

[*] See Bauer, *The National Question*, p. 422.

[†] See Springer, *The National Problem*, pp. 281-82.

point – the hub of the political life of Russia is not the national but the agrarian question. Consequently, the fate of the Russian problem, and, accordingly, the "liberation" of the nations too, is bound up in Russia with the solution of the agrarian question, i.e., with the destruction of the relics of feudalism, i.e., with the democratisation of the country. That explains why in Russia the national question is not an independent and decisive one, but a part of the general and more important question of the emancipation of the country.

"The barrenness of the Austrian parliament," writes Springer, "is due precisely to the fact that every reform gives rise to antagonisms within the national parties which may affect their unity. The leaders of the parties, therefore, avoid everything that smacks of reform. Progress in Austria is generally conceivable only if the nations are granted indefeasible legal rights which will relieve them of the necessity of constantly maintaining national militant groups in parliament and will enable them to turn their attention to the solution of economic and social problems."[*]

Bauer says the same thing.

"National peace is indispensable first of all for the state. The state cannot permit legislation to be brought to a standstill by the very stupid question of language or by every quarrel between excited people on a linguistic frontier, or over every new school."[†]

All this is clear. But it is no less clear that the national question in Russia is on an entirely different plane. It is not the national, but the agrarian question that decides the fate of progress in Russia. The national question is a subordinate one.

And so we have different presentations of the question, different prospects and methods of struggle, different immediate tasks. Is it not clear that, such being the state of affairs, only pedants who "solve" the national question without reference to space and time can think of adopting examples from Austria and of borrowing a programme?

To repeat: the concrete historical conditions as the starting point, and the dialectical presentation of the question as the only correct way of presenting it – such is the key to solving the national question.

---

[*] See Springer, *The National Problem*, p. 36.

[†] See Bauer, *The National Question*, p. 401.

IV

CULTURAL-NATIONAL AUTONOMY

We spoke above of the formal aspect of the Austrian national programme and of the methodological grounds which make it impossible for the Russian Marxists simply to adopt the example of Austrian Social-Democracy and make the latter's programme their own.

Let us now examine the essence of the programme itself.

What then is the national programme of the Austrian Social-Democrats?

It is expressed in two words: cultural-national autonomy.

This means, firstly, that autonomy would be granted, let us say, not to Bohemia or Poland, which are inhabited mainly by Czechs and Poles, but to Czechs and Poles generally, irrespective of territory, no matter what part of Austria they inhabit.

That is why this autonomy is called *national* and not territorial.

It means, secondly, that the Czechs, Poles, Germans, and so on, scattered over the various parts of Austria, taken personally, as individuals, are to be organised into integral nations, and are as such to form part of the Austrian state. In this way Austria would represent not a union of autonomous regions, but a union of autonomous nationalities, constituted irrespective of territory.

It means, thirdly, that the national institutions which are to be created for this purpose for the Poles, Czechs, and so forth, are to have jurisdiction only over "cultural," not "political" questions. Specifically political questions would be reserved for the Austrian parliament (the Reichsrat).

That is why this autonomy is also called *cultural*, cultural-national autonomy.

And here is the text of the programme adopted by the Austrian Social-Democratic Party at the Brünn Congress in 1899.[*]

Having referred to the fact that "national dissension in Austria is hindering political progress," that "the final solution of the national question... is primarily a cultural necessity," and that "the solution is possible only in a genuinely democratic society, con-

---

[*] The representatives of the South-Slav Social-Democratic Party also voted for it. See *Discussion of the National Question at the Brünn Congress*, 1906, p. 72.

structed on the basis of universal, direct and equal suffrage," the programme goes on to say:

*"The preservation and development of the national peculiarities** of the peoples of Austria is possible only on the basis of equal rights and by avoiding all oppression. Hence, all bureaucratic state centralism and the feudal privileges of individual provinces must first of all be rejected.

"Under these conditions, and only under these conditions, will it be possible to establish national order in Austria in place of national dissension, namely, on the following principles:

"1. Austria must be transformed into a democratic state federation of nationalities.

"2. The historical crown provinces must be replaced by nationally delimited self-governing corporations, in each of which legislation and administration shall be entrusted to national parliaments elected on the basis of universal, direct and equal suffrage.

"3. All the self-governing regions of one and the same nation must jointly form a single national union, which shall manage its national affairs on an absolutely autonomous basis.

"4. The rights of national minorities must be guaranteed by a special law passed by the Imperial Parliament."

The programme ends with an appeal for the solidarity of all the nations of Austria.[†]

It is not difficult to see that this programme retains certain traces of "territorialism," but that in general it gives a formulation of national autonomy. It is not without good reason that Springer, the first agitator on behalf of cultural-national autonomy, greets it with enthusiasm;[‡] Bauer also supports this programme, calling it a "theoretical victory"[§] for national autonomy; only, in the interests of greater clarity, he proposes that Point 4 be replaced by a more defi-

---

[*] In M. Panin's Russian translation (see his translation of Bauer's book), "national individualities" is given in place of "national peculiarities." Panin translated this passage incorrectly. The word "individuality" is not in the German text, which speaks of nationalen Eigenart, i.e., peculiarities, which is far from being the same thing.

[†] *Verhandlungen des Gesamtparteitages* in Brünn, 1899.

[‡] See Springer, *The National Problem*, p. 286.

[§] See *The National Question*, p. 549.

nite formulation, which would declare the necessity of "constituting the national minority within each self-governing region into a public corporation" for the management of educational and other cultural affairs.[*]

Such is the national programme of Austrian Social Democracy.

Let us examine its scientific foundations.

Let us see how the Austrian Social-Democratic Party justifies the cultural-national autonomy it advocates.

Let us turn to the theoreticians of cultural-national autonomy, Springer and Bauer.

The starting point of national autonomy is the conception of a nation as a union of individuals without regard to a definite territory.

"Nationality," according to Springer, "is not essentially connected with territory"; nations are "autonomous unions of persons."[†]

Bauer also speaks of a nation as a "community of persons" which does not enjoy "exclusive sovereignty in any particular region."[‡]

But the persons constituting a nation do not always live in one compact mass; they are frequently divided into groups, and in that form are interspersed among alien national organisms. It is capitalism which drives them into various regions and cities in search of a livelihood. But when they enter foreign national territories and there form minorities, these groups are made to suffer by the local national majorities in the way of restrictions on their language, schools, etc. Hence national conflicts. Hence the "unsuitability" of territorial autonomy. The only solution to such a situation, according to Springer and Bauer, is to organise the minorities of the given nationality dispersed over various parts of the state into a single, general, inter-class national union. Such a union alone, in their opinion, can protect the cultural interests of national minorities, and it alone is capable of putting an end to national discord.

"Hence the necessity," says Springer, "to organise the nationalities, to invest them with rights and responsibilities...."[*] Of course, "a law is easily drafted, but will it be effective?".... "If one wants to

---

[*] *Ibid.*, p. 555.

[†] See Springer, *The National Problem*, p. 19.

[‡] See *The National Question*, p. 286.

make a law for nations, one must first create the nations...."[†]
"Unless the nationalities are constituted it is impossible to create national rights and eliminate national dissension."[‡]

Bauer expressed himself in the same spirit when he proposed, as "a demand of the working class," that "the minorities should be constituted into public corporations based on the personal principle."[§]

But how is a nation to be organised? How is one to determine to what nation any given individual belongs?

"Nationality," says Springer, "will be determined by certificates; every individual domiciled in a given region must declare his affiliation to one of the nationalities of that region."[**]

"The personal principle," says Bauer, "presumes that the population will be divided into nationalities.... On the basis of the free declaration of the adult citizens national registers must be drawn up."[††]

Further.

"All the Germans in nationally homogeneous districts," says Bauer, "and all the Germans entered in the national registers in the dual districts will constitute the German nation and elect a *National Council*."[‡‡]

The same applies to the Czechs, Poles, and so on.

"The *National Council*," according to Springer, "is the cultural parliament of the nation, empowered to establish the principles and to grant funds, thereby assuming guardianship over national education, national literature, art and science, the formation of academies, museums, galleries, theatres," etc.[§§]

Such will be the organisation of a nation and its central institution. According to Bauer, the Austrian Social-Democratic Party is

---

[*] See *The National Problem*, p. 74.

[†] *Ibid.*, pp. 88-89.

[‡] *Ibid.*, p. 89.

[§] See *The National Question*, p. 552.

[**] See *The National Problem*, p. 226.

[††] See *The National Question*, p. 368.

[‡‡] *Ibid.*, p. 375.

[§§] See *The National Problem*, p. 234.

striving, by the creation of these inter-class institutions "to make national culture... the possession of the whole people and thereby *unite all the members of the nation into a national-cultural commu-nity*"[*] (our italics).

One might think that all this concerns Austria alone. But Bauer does not agree. He emphatically declares that national autonomy is essential also for other states which, like Austria, consist of several nationalities.

"In the multi-national state," according to Bauer, "the working class of all the nations opposes the national power policy of the propertied classes with the demand for national autonomy."[†]

Then, imperceptibly substituting national autonomy for the self-determination of nations, he continues:

"Thus, national autonomy, the self-determination of nations, will necessarily become the constitutional programme of the prole-tariat of all the nations in a multi-national state."[‡]

But he goes still further. He profoundly believes that the inter-class "national unions" "constituted" by him and Springer will serve as a sort of prototype of the future socialist society. For he knows that "the socialist system of society... will divide humanity into na-tionally delimited communities";[§] that under socialism there will take place "a grouping of humanity into autonomous national com-munities,"[**] that thus, "socialist society will undoubtedly present a checkered picture of national unions of persons and territorial cor-porations,"[††] and that accordingly "the socialist principle of ity is a higher synthesis of the national principle and national auton-omy."[‡‡]

Enough, it would seem....

These are the arguments for cultural-national autonomy as given in the works of Bauer and Springer.

---

[*] See *The National Question*, p. 553.

[†] See *Ibid.*, p. 337.

[‡] See *The National Question*, p. 333.

[§] *Ibid.*, p. 555.

[**] See *Ibid.*, p. 556.

[††] See *Ibid.*, p. 543.

[‡‡] See *Ibid.*, p. 542.

The first thing that strikes the eye is the entirely inexplicable and absolutely unjustifiable substitution of national autonomy for self-determination of nations. One or the other: either Bauer failed to understand the meaning of self-determination, or he did understand it but for some reason or other deliberately narrowed its meaning. For there is no doubt a) that cultural-national autonomy presupposes the integrity of the multi-national state, whereas self-determination goes outside the framework of this integrity, and b) that self-determination endows a nation with complete rights, whereas national autonomy endows it only with "cultural" rights. That in the first place.

In the second place, a combination of internal and external conditions is fully possible at some future time by virtue of which one or another of the nationalities may decide to secede from a multinational state, say from Austria. Did not the Ruthenian Social-Democrats at the Brünn Party Congress announce their readiness to unite the "two parts" of their people into one whole?[*] What, in such such a case, becomes of national autonomy, which is *"inevitable for the proletariat of all the nations"*? What sort of "solution" of the problem is it that mechanically squeezes nations into the Procrustean bed of an integral state?

Further: National autonomy is contrary to the whole course of development of nations. It calls for the organisation of nations; but can they be artificially welded together if life, if economic development tears whole groups from them and disperses these groups over various regions? There is no doubt that in the early stages of capitalism nations become welded together. But there is also no doubt that in the higher stages of capitalism a process of dispersion of nations sets in, a process whereby a whole number of groups separate off from the nations, going off in search of a livelihood and subsequently settling permanently in other regions of the state; in the course of this these settlers lose their old connections and acquire new ones in their new domicile, and from generation to generation acquire new habits and new tastes, and possibly a new language. The question arises: is it possible to unite into a single national union groups that have grown so distinct? Where are the magic links to unite what cannot be united? Is it conceivable that,

---

[*] See *Proceedings of the Brünn Social-Democratic Party Congress*, p. 48.

for instance, the Germans of the Baltic Provinces and the Germans of Transcaucasia can be "united into a single nation"? But if it is not conceivable and not possible, wherein does national autonomy differ from the utopia of the old nationalists, who endeavoured to turn back the wheel of history?

But the unity of a nation diminishes not only as a result of migration. It diminishes also from internal causes, owing to the growing acuteness of the class struggle. In the early stages of capitalism one can still speak of a "common culture" of the proletariat and the bourgeoisie. But as large-scale industry develops and the class struggle becomes more and more acute, this "common culture" begins to melt away. One cannot seriously speak of the "common culture" of a nation when employers and workers of one and the same nation cease to understand each other. What "common destiny" can there be when the bourgeoisie thirsts for war, and the proletariat declares "war on war"? Can a single inter-class national union be formed from such opposed elements? And, after this, can one speak of the "union of all the members of the nation into a national-cultural community"?[*] Is it not obvious that national autonomy is contrary to the whole course of the class struggle?

But let us assume for a moment that the slogan "organise the nation" is practicable. One might understand bourgeois-nationalist parliamentarians endeavouring to "organise" a nation for the purpose of securing addition al votes. But since when have Social-Democrats begun to occupy themselves with "organising" nations, "constituting" nations, "creating" nations?

What sort of Social-Democrats are they who in the epoch of extreme intensification of the class struggle organise inter-class national unions? Until now the Austrian, as well as every other, Social-Democratic Party, had one task before it: namely, to organise the proletariat. That task has apparently become "antiquated." Springer and Bauer are now setting a "new" task, a more absorbing task, namely, to "create," to "organise" a nation.

However, logic has its obligations: he who adopts national autonomy must also adopt this "new" task; but to adopt the latter means to abandon the class position and to take the path of nationalism.

---

[*] Bauer, *The National Question*, p. 553

Springer's and Bauer's cultural-national autonomy is a subtle form of nationalism.

And it is by no means fortuitous that the national programme of the Austrian Social-Democrats enjoins a concern for the "*preservation* and *development* of the national peculiarities of the peoples." Just think: to "preserve" such "national peculiarities" of the Transcaucasian Tatars as self-flagellation at the festival of *Shakhsei-Vakhsei*; or to "develop" such "national peculiarities" of the Georgians as the vendetta!...

A demand of this character is in place in an outright bourgeois nationalist programme; and if it appears in the programme of the Austrian Social-Democrats it is because national autonomy tolerates such demands, it does not contradict them.

But if national autonomy is unsuitable now, it will be still more unsuitable in the future, socialist society.

Bauer's prophecy regarding the "division of humanity into nationally delimited communities"[*] is refuted by the whole course of development of modern human society. National barriers are being demolished and are falling, rather than becoming firmer. As early as the 'forties Marx declared that "national differences and antagonisms between peoples are daily more and more vanishing" and that "the supremacy of the proletariat will cause them to vanish still faster."[5] The subsequent development of mankind, accompanied as it was by the colossal growth of capitalist production, the reshuffling of nationalities and the union of people within ever larger territories, emphatically confirms Marx's thought.

Bauer's desire to represent socialist society as a "checkered picture of national unions of persons and territorial corporations" is a timid attempt to substitute for Marx's conception of socialism a revised version of Bakunin's conception. The history of socialism proves that every such attempt contains the elements of inevitable failure.

There is no need to mention the kind of "socialist principle of nationality" glorified by Bauer, which, in our opinion, substitutes for the socialist principle of the *class struggle* the bourgeois "*principle of nationality*." If national autonomy is based on such a dubious principle, it must be admitted that it can only cause harm to the working-class movement.

---

[*] See the beginning of this chapter.

True, such nationalism is not so transparent, for it is skilfully masked by socialist phrases, but it is all the more harmful to the proletariat for that reason. We can always cope with open nationalism, for it can easily be discerned. It is much more difficult to combat nationalism when it is masked and unrecognisable beneath its mask. Protected by the armour of socialism, it is less vulnerable and more tenacious. Implanted among the workers, it poisons the atmosphere and spreads harmful ideas of mutual distrust and segregation among the workers of the different nationalities.

But this does not exhaust the harm caused by national autonomy. It prepares the ground not only for the segregation of nations, but also for breaking up the united labour movement. The idea of national autonomy creates the psychological conditions for the division of the united workers' party into separate parties built on national lines. The break-up of the party is followed by the break-up of the trade unions, and complete segregation is the result. In this way the united class movement is broken up into separate national rivulets.

Austria, the home of "national autonomy," provides the most deplorable examples of this. As early as 1897 the Wimberg Party Congress[6]) the once united Austrian Social-Democratic Party began to break up into separate parties. The break-up became still more marked after the Brünn Party Congress (1899), which adopted national autonomy. Matters have finally come to such a pass that in place of a united international party there are now six national parties, of which the Czech Social-Democratic Party will not even have anything to do with the German Social-Democratic Party.

But with the parties are associated the trade unions. In Austria, both in the parties and in the trade unions, the main brunt of the work is borne by the same Social-Democratic workers. There was therefore reason to fear that separatism in the party would lead to separatism in the trade unions and that the trade unions would also break up. That, in fact, is what happened: the trade unions have also divided according to nationality. Now things frequently go so far that the Czech workers will even break a strike of German workers, or will unite at municipal elections with the Czech bourgeois against the German workers.

It will be seen from the foregoing that cultural-national autonomy is no solution of the national question. Not only that, it serves to aggravate and confuse the question by creating a situation which favours the destruction of the unity of the labour movement, fosters the segregation of the workers according to nationality and intensifies friction among them. Such is the harvest of national autonomy.

V

THE BUND, ITS NATIONALISM, ITS SEPARATISM

We said above that Bauer, while granting the necessity of national autonomy for the Czechs, Poles, and so on, nevertheless opposes similar autonomy for the Jews. In answer to the question, "Should the working class demand autonomy for the Jewish people?" Bauer says that "national autonomy cannot be demanded by the Jewish workers."[*] According to Bauer, the reason is that "capitalist society makes it impossible for them (the Jews – *J. St.*) to continue as a nation."[†]

In brief, the Jewish nation is coming to an end, and hence there is nobody to demand national autonomy for. The Jews are being assimilated.

This view of the fate of the Jews as a nation is not a new one. It was expressed by Marx as early as the 'forties,[‡][7] in reference chiefly to the German Jews. It was repeated by Kautsky in 1903,[§] in reference to the Russian Jews. It is now being repeated by Bauer in reference to the Austrian Jews, with the difference, however, that he denies not the present but the future of the Jewish nation.

Bauer explains the impossibility of preserving the existence of the Jews as a nation by the fact that "the Jews have no closed territory of settlement."[**] This explanation, in the main a correct one, does not however express the whole truth. The fact of the matter is primarily that among the Jews there is no large and stable stratum connected with the land, which would naturally rivet the nation together, serving not only as its framework but also as a "national" market. Of the five or six million Russian Jews, only three to four

---

[*] See *The National Question*, pp. 381, 396.

[†] *Ibid.*, p. 389.

[‡] See K. Marx, "The Jewish Question," 1906.

[§] See K. Kautsky, "The Kishinev Pogrom and the Jewish Question," 1903.

[**] See *The National Question*, p. 388.

per cent are connected with agriculture in any way. The remaining ninety-six per cent are employed in trade, industry, in urban institutions, and in general are town dwellers; moreover, they are spread all over Russia and do not constitute a majority in a single gubernia.

Thus, interspersed as national minorities in areas inhabited by other nationalities, the Jews as a rule serve "foreign" nations as manufacturers and traders and as members of the liberal professions, naturally adapting themselves to the "foreign nations" in respect to language and so forth. All this, taken together with the increasing re-shuffling of nationalities characteristic of developed forms of capitalism, leads to the assimilation of the Jews. The abolition of the "Pale of Settlement" would only serve to hasten this process of assimilation.

The question of national autonomy for the Russian Jews consequently assumes a somewhat curious character: autonomy is being proposed for a nation whose future is denied and whose existence has still to be proved!

Nevertheless, this was the curious and shaky position taken up by the Bund when at its Sixth Congress (1905) it adopted a "national programme" on the lines of national autonomy.

Two circumstances impelled the Bund to take this step.

The first circumstance is the existence of the Bund as an organisation of Jewish, and only Jewish, Social-Democratic workers. Even before 1897 the Social-Democratic groups active among the Jewish workers set themselves the aim of creating "a special Jewish workers' organisation."[*] They founded such an organisation in 1897 1897 by uniting to form the Bund. That was at a time when Russian Social-Democracy as an integral body virtually did not yet exist. The Bund steadily grew and spread, and stood out more and more vividly against the background of the bleak days of Russian Social Democracy.... Then came the 1900's. A *mass* labour movement came into being. Polish Social-Democracy grew and drew the Jewish workers into the mass struggle. Russian Social-Democracy grew and attracted the "Bund" workers. Lacking a territorial basis, the national framework of the Bund became too restrictive. The Bund was faced with the problem of either merging with the general in-

---

[*] See *Forms of the National Movement*, etc., edited by Kastelyansky, p. 772.

ternational tide, or of upholding its independent existence as an extra-territorial organisation. The Bund chose the latter course.

Thus grew up the "theory" that the Bund is "the sole representative of the Jewish proletariat."

But to justify this strange "theory" in any "simple" way became impossible. Some kind of foundation "on principle," some justification "on principle," was needed. Cultural-national autonomy provided such a foundation. The Bund seized upon it, borrowing it from the Austrian Social-Democrats. If the Austrians had not had such a programme the Bund would have invented it in order to justify its independent existence "on principle."

Thus, after a timid attempt in 1901 (the Fourth Congress), the Bund definitely adopted a "national programme" in 1905 (the Sixth Congress).

The second circumstance is the peculiar position of the Jews as separate national minorities within compact majorities of other nationalities in integral regions. We have already said that this position is undermining the existence of the Jews as a nation and puts them on the road to assimilation. But this is an objective process. Subjectively, in the minds of the Jews, it provokes a reaction and gives rise to the demand for a guarantee of the rights of a national minority, for a guarantee against assimilation. Preaching as it does the vitality of the Jewish "nationality," the Bund could not avoid being in favour of a "guarantee." And, having taken up this position, it could not but accept national autonomy. For if the Bund could seize upon any autonomy at all, it could only be national autonomy, i.e., *cultural-national* autonomy; there could be no question of territorial-political autonomy for the Jews, since the Jews have no definite integral territory.

It is noteworthy that the Bund from the outset stressed the character of national autonomy as a guarantee of the rights of national minorities, as a guarantee of the "free development" of nations. Nor was it fortuitous that the representative of the Bund at the Second Congress of the Russian Social-Democratic Party, Goldblatt, defined national autonomy as "institutions which *guarantee* them (i.e., nations – *J. St.*) complete freedom of cultural development."[*] A similar proposal was made by supporters of the ideas of the Bund to the Social-Democratic group in the Fourth Duma....

---

[*] See *Minutes of the Second Congress*, p. 176.

In this way the Bund adopted the curious position of national autonomy for the Jews.

We have examined above national autonomy in general. The examination showed that national autonomy leads to nationalism. We shall see later that the Bund has arrived at the same end point. But the Bund also regards national autonomy from a special aspect, namely, from the aspect of *guarantees* of the rights of national minorities. Let us also examine the question from this special aspect. It is all the more necessary since the problem of national minorities – and not of the Jewish minorities alone – is one of serious moment for Social-Democracy.

And so, it is a question of "institutions which guarantee" nations "complete freedom of cultural development" (our italics – *J. St.*).

But what are these "institutions which guarantee," etc.?

They are primarily the "National Council" of Springer and Bauer, something in the nature of a Diet for cultural affairs.

But can these institutions guarantee a nation "complete freedom of cultural development"? Can a Diet for cultural affairs guarantee a nation against nationalist persecution?

The Bund believes it can.

But history proves the contrary.

At one time a Diet existed in Russian Poland. It was a political Diet and, of course, endeavoured to guarantee freedom of "cultural development" for the Poles. But, far from succeeding in doing so, it itself succumbed in the unequal struggle against the political conditions generally prevailing in Russia.

A Diet has been in existence for a long time in Finland, and it too endeavours to protect the Finnish nationality from "encroachments," but how far it succeeds in doing so everybody can see.

Of course, there are Diets and Diets, and it is not so easy to cope with the democratically organised Finnish Diet as it was with the aristocratic Polish Diet. But the decisive factor, nevertheless, is not the Diet, but the general regime in Russia. If such a grossly Asiatic social and political regime existed in Russia now as in the past, at the time the Polish Diet was abolished, things would go much harder with the Finnish Diet. Moreover, the policy of "encroachments" upon Finland is growing, and it cannot be said that it has met with defeat....

If such is the case with old, historically evolved institutions – political Diets – still less will young Diets, young institutions, especially such feeble institutions as "cultural" Diets, be able to guarantee the free development of nations.

Obviously, it is not a question of "institutions," but of the general regime prevailing in the country. If there is no democracy in the country there can be no guarantees of "complete freedom for cultural development" of nationalities. One may say with certainty that the more democratic a country is the fewer are the "encroachments" made on the "freedom of nationalities," and the greater are the guarantees against such "encroachments."

Russia is a semi-Asiatic country, and therefore in Russia the policy of "encroachments" not infrequently assumes the grossest form, the form of pogroms. It need hardly be said that in Russia "guarantees" have been reduced to the very minimum.

Germany is, however, European, and she enjoys a measure of political freedom. It is not surprising that the policy of "encroachments" there never takes the form of pogroms.

In France, of course, there are still more "guarantees," for France is more democratic than Germany.

There is no need to mention Switzerland, where, thanks to her highly developed, although bourgeois democracy, nationalities live in freedom, whether they are a minority or a majority.

Thus the Bund adopts a false position when it asserts that "institutions" by themselves are able to guarantee complete cultural development for nationalities.

It may be said that the Bund itself regards the establishment of democracy in Russia as a *preliminary* condition for the "creation of institutions" and guarantees of freedom. But this is not the case. From the report of the Eighth Conference of the Bund[8] it will be seen that the Bund thinks it can secure "institutions" *on the basis* of the present system in Russia, by "reforming" the *Jewish community*.

"The community," one of the leaders of the Bund said at this conference, "may become the nucleus of future cultural-national autonomy. Cultural-national autonomy is a form of self-service on the part of nations, a form of satisfying national needs. The community form conceals within itself a similar content. They are links in the same chain, stages in the same evolution."*

---

* *Report of the Eighth Conference of the Bund*, 1911, p. 62.

On this basis, the conference decided that it was necessary to strive "for *reforming* the Jewish community and transforming it by *legislative means* into a secular institution," democratically organised* (our italics – *J. St.*).

It is evident that the Bund considers as the condition and guarantee not the democratisation of Russia, but some future "secular institution" of the Jews, obtained by "reforming the Jewish community," so to speak, by "legislative" means, through the Duma.

But we have already seen that "institutions" in themselves cannot serve as "guarantees" if the regime in the state generally is not a democratic one.

But what, it may be asked, will be the position under a future democratic system? Will not special "cultural institutions which guarantee," etc., be required even under democracy? What is the position in this respect in democratic Switzerland, for example? Are there special cultural institutions in Switzerland on the pattern of Springer's "National Council"? No, there are *not*. But do not the cultural interests of, for instance, the Italians, who constitute a minority there, suffer for that reason? One does not seem to hear that they do. And that is quite natural: in Switzerland all special cultural "institutions," which supposedly "guarantee," etc., are rendered superfluous by democracy.

And so, impotent in the present and superfluous in the future – such are the *institutions* of cultural-national autonomy, and such is national autonomy.

But it becomes still more harmful when it is thrust upon a "nation" whose existence and future are open to doubt. In such cases the advocates of national autonomy are obliged to protect and preserve all the peculiar features of the "nation," the bad as well as the good, just for the sake of "saving the nation" from assimilation, just for the sake of "preserving" it.

That the Bund should take this dangerous path was inevitable. And it did take it. We are referring to the resolutions of recent conferences of the Bund on the question of the "Sabbath," "Yiddish," etc.

Social-Democracy strives to secure *for all nations* the right to use their own language. But that does not satisfy the Bund; it demands that "the rights of the *Jewish* language" (our italics – *J. St.*)

---

* *Ibid.*, pp. 83-84.

be championed with "exceptional persistence,"[*] and the Bund itself in the elections to the Fourth Duma declared that it would give "preference to those of them (i.e., electors) who undertake to defend the rights of the Jewish language."[†]

Not the *general* right of all nations to use their own language, but the *particular* right of the Jewish language, Yiddish! Let the workers of the various nationalities fight *primarily* for their own language: the Jews for Jewish, the Georgians for Georgian, and so forth. The struggle for the general right of all nations is a secondary matter. You do not have to recognise the right of all oppressed nationalities to use their own language; but if you have recognised the right of Yiddish, know that the Bund will vote for you, the Bund will "prefer" you.

But in what way then does the Bund differ from the bourgeois nationalists?

Social-Democracy strives to secure the establishment of a compulsory weekly rest day. But that does not satisfy the Bund; it demands that "by legislative means" "the Jewish proletariat should be guaranteed the right to observe their Sabbath and be relieved of the obligation to observe another day."[‡]

It is to be expected that the Bund will take another "step forward" and demand the right to observe all the ancient Hebrew holidays. And if, to the misfortune of the Bund, the Jewish workers have discarded religious prejudices and do not want to observe these holidays, the Bund with its agitation for "the right to the Sabbath," will remind them of the Sabbath, it will, so to speak, cultivate among them "the Sabbatarian spirit."...

Quite comprehensible, therefore, are the "passionate speeches" delivered at the Eighth Conference of the Bund demanding "Jewish hospitals," a demand that was based on the argument that "a patient feels more at home among his own people," that "the Jewish worker will not feel at ease among Polish workers, but will feel at ease among Jewish shopkeepers."[§]

---

[*] See *Report of the Eighth Conference of the Bund*, p. 85.

[†] See *Report of the Ninth Conference of the Bund*, 1912, p. 42.

[‡] See *Report of the Eighth Conference of the Bund*, p. 83

[§] *Ibid.*, p. 68.

Preservation of everything Jewish, conservation of all the national peculiarities of the Jews, even those that are patently harmful to the proletariat, isolation of the Jews from everything non-Jewish, even the establishment of special hospitals – that is the level to which the Bund has sunk!

Comrade Plekhanov was right a thousand times over when he said that the Bund "is adapting socialism to nationalism." Of course, V. Kossovsky and Bundists like him may denounce Plekhanov as a "demagogue"[*][9] – paper will put up with anything that is written on it – but those who are familiar with the activities of the Bund will easily realise that these brave fellows are simply afraid to tell the truth about themselves and are hiding behind strong language about "demagogy."...

But since it holds such a position on the national question, the Bund was naturally obliged, in the matter of organisation also, to take the path of segregating the Jewish workers, the path of formation of national *curiae* within Social-Democracy. Such is the logic of national autonomy!

And, in fact, the Bund did pass from the theory of sole representation to the theory of "national demarcation" of workers. The Bund demands that Russian Social-Democracy should "in its organisational structure introduce demarcation according to nationalities."[†] From "demarcation" it made a "step forward" to the theory of "segregation." It is not for nothing that speeches were made at the Eighth Conference of the Bund declaring that "national existence lies in segregation."[‡]

Organisational federalism harbours the elements of disintegration and separatism. The Bund is heading for separatism.

And, indeed, there is nothing else it can head for. Its very existence as an extra-territorial organisation drives it to separatism. The Bund does not possess a definite integral territory; it operates on "foreign" territories, whereas the neighbouring Polish, Lettish and Russian Social-Democracies are international territorial collective bodies. But the result is that every extension of these collective bod-

---

[*] See *Nasha Zarya*, No. 9-10, 1912, p. 120.

[†] See *An Announcement on the Seventh Congress of the Bund*,[10] p. 7.

[‡] See *Report of the Eighth Conference of the Bund*, p. 72.

ies means a "loss" to the Bund and a restriction of its field of action. There are two alternatives: either Russian Social-Democracy as a whole must be reconstructed on the basis of national federalism – which will enable the Bund to "secure" the Jewish proletariat for itself; or the territorial-international principle of these collective bodies remains in force – in which case the Bund must be reconstructed on the basis of internationalism, as is the case with the Polish and Lettish Social-Democracies.

This explains why the Bund from the very beginning demanded "the reorganisation of Russian Social-Democracy on a federal basis."[*]

In 1906, yielding to the pressure from below in favour of unity, the Bund chose a middle path and joined Russian Social-Democracy. But how did it join? Whereas the Polish and Lettish Social-Democracies joined for the purpose of peaceable joint action, the Bund joined for the purpose of waging war for a federation. That is exactly what Medem, the leader of the Bundists, said at the time:

"We are joining not for the sake of an idyll, but in order to fight. There is no idyll, and only Manilovs could hope for one in the near future. The Bund must join the Party armed from head to foot."[†]

It would be wrong to regard this as an expression of evil intent on Medem's part. It is not a matter of evil intent, but of the peculiar position of the Bund, which compels it to fight Russian Social-Democracy, which is built on the basis of internationalism. And in fighting it the Bund naturally violated the interests of unity. Finally, matters went so far that the Bund formally broke with Russian Social-Democracy, violating its statutes, and in the elections to the Fourth Duma joining forces with the Polish nationalists against the Polish Social-Democrats.

The Bund has apparently found that a rupture is the best guarantee for independent activity. And so the "principle" of organisational "demarcation" led to separatism and to a complete rupture.

---

[*] See *Concerning National Autonomy and the Reorganisation of Russian Social-Democracy on a Federal Basis*, 1902, published by the Bund.

[†] *Nashe Slovo*, No. 3, Vilno, 1906, p. 24.

In a controversy with the old *Iskra*[11] on the question of federalism, the Bund once wrote:

"*Iskra* wants to assure us that federal relations between the Bund and Russian Social-Democracy are bound to weaken the ties between them. We cannot refute this opinion by referring to practice in Russia, for the simple reason that Russian Social-Democracy does not exist as a federal body. But we can refer to the extremely instructive experience of Social-Democracy in Austria, which assumed a federal character by virtue of the decision of the Party Congress of 1897."*

That was written in 1902.

But we are now in the year 1913. We now have both Russian "practice" and the "experience of Social-Democracy in Austria."

What do they tell us?

Let us begin with "the extremely instructive experience of Social-Democracy in Austria." Up to 1896 there was a united Social-Democratic Party in Austria. In that year the Czechs at the International Congress in London for the first time demanded separate representation, and were given it. In 1897, at the Vienna (Wimberg) Party Congress, the united party was formally liquidated and in its place a federal league of six national "Social-Democratic groups" was set up. Subsequently these "groups" were converted into independent parties, which gradually severed contact with one another. Following the parties, the parliamentary group broke up – national "clubs" were formed. Next came the trade unions, which also split according to nationalities. Even the co-operative societies were affected, the Czech separatists calling upon the workers to split them up.† We will not dwell on the fact that separatist agitation weakens the workers' sense of solidarity and frequently drives them to strike-breaking.

Thus "the extremely instructive experience of Social Democracy in Austria" speaks *against* the Bund and for the old *Iskra*. Federalism in the Austrian party has led to the most outrageous separatism, to the destruction of the unity of the labour movement.

---

* *National Autonomy*, etc., 1902, p. 17, published by the Bund.

† See the words quoted from a brochure by Vanêk[12] in *Dokumente des Separatismus*, p. 29.

We have seen above that "practical experience in Russia" also bears this out. Like the Czech separatists, the Bundist separatists have broken with the general Russian Social-Democratic Party. As for the trade unions, the Bundist trade unions, from the outset they were organised on national lines, that is to say, they were cut off from the workers of other nationalities.

Complete segregation and complete rupture – that is what is revealed by the "Russian practical experience" of federalism.

It is not surprising that the effect of this state of affairs upon the workers is to weaken their sense of solidarity and to demoralise them; and the latter process is also penetrating the Bund. We are referring to the increasing collisions between Jewish and Polish workers in connection with unemployment. Here is the kind of speech that was made on this subject at the Ninth Conference of the Bund:

"...We regard the Polish workers, who are ousting us, as pogromists, as scabs; we do not support their strikes, we break them. Secondly, we reply to being ousted by ousting in our turn: we reply to Jewish workers not being allowed into the factories by not allowing Polish workers near the benches.... *If we do not take this matter into our own hands the workers will follow others*"[*] (our italics – *J. St.*).

That is the way they talk about solidarity at a Bundist conference.

You cannot go further than that in the way of "demarcation" and "segregation." The Bund has achieved its aim: it is carrying its demarcation between the workers of different nationalities to the point of conflicts and strike-breaking. And there is no other course: "If we do not take this matter into our own hands *the workers will follow others....*"

Disorganisation of the labour movement, demoralisation of the Social-Democratic ranks – that is what the federalism of the Bund leads to.

Thus the idea of cultural-national autonomy, the atmosphere it creates, has proved to be even more harmful in Russia than in Austria.

---

[*] See *Report of the Ninth Conference of the Bund*, p. 19.

VI

THE CAUCASIANS, THE CONFERENCE
OF THE LIQUIDATORS

We spoke above of the waverings of one section of the Caucasian Social-Democrats who were unable to withstand the nationalist "epidemic." These waverings were revealed in the fact that, strange as it may seem, the above-mentioned Social-Democrats followed in the footsteps of the Bund and proclaimed cultural-national autonomy.

Regional autonomy for the Caucasus as a whole and cultural-national autonomy for the nations forming the Caucasus – that is the way these Social-Democrats, who, incidentally, are linked with the Russian Liquidators, formulate their demand.

Listen to their acknowledged leader, the not unknown *N*.

"Everybody knows that the Caucasus differs profoundly from the central gubernias, both as regards the racial composition of its population and as regards its territory and agricultural development. The exploitation and material development of such a region require local workers acquainted with local peculiarities and accustomed to the local climate and culture. All laws designed to further the exploitation of the local territory should be issued locally and put into effect by local forces. Consequently, the jurisdiction of the central organ of Caucasian self-government should extend to legislation on local questions.... Hence, the functions of the Caucasian centre should consist in the passing of laws designed to further the economic exploitation of the local territory and the material prosperity of the region."[*]

Thus – regional autonomy for the Caucasus.

If we abstract ourselves from the rather confused and incoherent arguments of *N*., it must be admitted that his conclusion is correct. Regional autonomy for the Caucasus, within the framework of a general state constitution, which *N*. does not deny, is indeed essential because of the peculiarities of its composition and its conditions of life. This was also acknowledged by the Russian Social-Democratic Party, which at its Second Congress proclaimed "regional self-government for those border regions which in respect of

---

[*] See the Georgian newspaper *Chveni Tskhovreba* (*Our Life*),[13] No. 12, 1912.

their conditions of life and the composition of their population differ from the regions of Russia proper."

When Martov submitted this point for discussion at the Second Congress, he justified it on the grounds that "the vast extent of Russia and the experience of our centralised administration point to the necessity and expediency of regional self-government for such large units as Finland, Poland, Lithuania and the Caucasus."

But it follows that regional *self-government* is to be interpreted as regional *autonomy*.

But *N.* goes further. According to him, regional autonomy for the Caucasus covers "only one aspect of the question."

"So far we have spoken only of the material development of local life. But the economic development of a region is facilitated not only by economic activity but also by spiritual, cultural activity."... "A culturally strong nation is strong also in the economic sphere."... "But the cultural development of nations is possible only in the national languages."... "Consequently, all questions connected with the native language are questions of national culture. Such are the questions of education, the judicature, the church, literature, art, science, the theatre, etc. If the material development of a region unites nations, matters of national culture disunite them and place each in a separate sphere. Activities of the former kind are associated with a definite territory."... "This is not the case with matters of national culture. These are associated not with a definite territory but with the existence of a definite nation. The fate of the Georgian language interests a Georgian, no matter where he lives. It would be a sign of profound ignorance to say that Georgian culture concerns only the Georgians who live in Georgia. Take, for instance, the Armenian church. Armenians of various localities and states take part in the administration of its affairs. Territory plays no part here. Or, for instance, the creation of a Georgian museum interests not only the Georgians of Tiflis, but also the Georgians of Baku, Kutais, St. Petersburg, etc. Hence, the administration and control of all affairs of national culture must be left to the nations concerned. We proclaim in favour of cultural-national autonomy for the Caucasian nationalities."[*]

---

[*] See the Georgian newspaper *Chveni Tskhovreba*, No. 12, 1912.

In short, since culture is not territory, and territory is not culture, cultural-national autonomy is required. That is all *N.* can say in the latter's favour.

We shall not stop to discuss again national-cultural autonomy in general; we have already spoken of its objectionable character. We should like to point out only that, while being unsuitable in general, cultural-national autonomy is also meaningless and nonsensical in relation to Caucasian conditions.

And for the following reason:

Cultural-national autonomy presumes more or less developed nationalities, with a developed culture and literature. Failing these conditions, autonomy loses all sense and becomes an absurdity. But in the Caucasus there are a number of nationalities each possessing a primitive culture, a separate language, but without its own literature; nationalities, moreover, which are in a state of transition, partly becoming assimilated and partly continuing to develop. How is cultural-national autonomy to be applied to them? What is to be done with such nationalities? How are they to be "organised" into separate cultural-national unions, as is undoubtedly implied by cultural-national autonomy?

What is to be done with the Mingrelians, the Abkhasians, the Adjarians, the Svanetians, the Lesghians, and so on, who speak different languages but do not possess a literature of their own? To what nations are they to be attached? Can they be "organised" into national unions? Around what "cultural affairs" are they to be "organised"?

What is to be done with the Ossetians, of whom the Transcaucasian Ossetians are becoming assimilated (but are as yet by no means wholly assimilated) by the Georgians while the Cis-Caucasian Ossetians are partly being assimilated by the Russians and partly continuing to develop and are creating their own literature? How are they to be "organised" into a single national union?

To what national union should one attach the Adjarians, who speak the Georgian language, but whose culture is Turkish and who profess the religion of Islam? Shall they be "organised" separately from the Georgians *with regard to religious affairs* and together with the Georgians *with regard to other cultural affairs*? And what about the Kobuletians, the Ingushes, the Inghilois?

What kind of autonomy is that which excludes a whole number of nationalities from the list?

No, that is not a solution of the national question, but the fruit of idle fancy.

But let us grant the impossible and assume that our *N*.'s national-cultural autonomy has been put into effect. Where would it lead to, what would be its results? Take, for instance, the Transcaucasian Tatars, with their minimum percentage of literates, their schools controlled by the omnipotent mullahs and their culture permeated by the religious spirit.... It is not difficult to understand that to "organise" them into a cultural national union would mean to place them under the control of the mullahs, to deliver them over to the tender mercies of the reactionary mullahs, to create a new stronghold of spiritual enslavement of the Tatar masses to their worst enemy.

But since when have Social-Democrats made it a practice to bring grist to the mill of the reactionaries?

Could the Caucasian Liquidators really find nothing better to "proclaim" than the isolation of the Transcaucasian Tatars within a cultural-national union which would place the masses under the thraldom of vicious reactionaries?

No, that is no solution of the national question.

The national question in the Caucasus can be solved only *by drawing the belated nations and nationalities into the common stream of a higher culture*. It is the only progressive solution and the only solution acceptable to Social-Democracy. Regional autonomy in the Caucasus is acceptable because it would draw the belated nations into the common cultural development; it would help them to cast off the shell of small-nation insularity; it would impel them forward and facilitate access to the benefits of higher culture. Cultural-national autonomy, however, acts in a diametrically opposite direction, because it shuts up the nations within their old shells, binds them to the lower stages of cultural development and prevents them from rising to the higher stages of culture.

In this way national autonomy counteracts the beneficial aspects of regional autonomy and nullifies it.

That is why the mixed type of autonomy which combines national-cultural autonomy and regional autonomy as proposed by *N*. is also unsuitable. This unnatural combination does not improve matters but makes them worse, because in addition to retarding the development of the belated nations it transforms regional autonomy into an arena of conflict between the nations organised in the national unions.

Thus cultural-national autonomy, which is unsuitable generally, would be a senseless, reactionary undertaking in the Caucasus.

So much for the cultural-national autonomy of *N.* and his Caucasian fellow-thinkers.

Whether the Caucasian Liquidators will take "a step forward" and follow in the footsteps of the Bund on the question of organisation also, the future will show. So far, in the history of Social-Democracy federalism in organisation always preceded national autonomy in programme. The Austrian Social-Democrats introduced organisational federalism as far back as 1897, and it was only two years later (1899) that they adopted national autonomy. The Bundists spoke distinctly of national autonomy for the first time in 1901, whereas organisational federalism had been practised by them since 1897.

The Caucasian Liquidators have begun from the end, from national autonomy. If they continue to follow in the footsteps of the Bund they will first have to demolish the whole existing organisational edifice, which was erected at the end of the 'nineties on the basis of internationalism.

But, easy though it was to adopt national autonomy, which is still not understood by the workers, it will be difficult to demolish an edifice which it has taken years to build and which has been raised and cherished by the workers of all the nationalities of the Caucasus. This Herostratian undertaking has only to be begun and the eyes of the workers will be opened to the nationalist character of cultural-national autonomy.

———

While the Caucasians are settling the national question in the usual manner, by means of verbal and written discussion, the All-Russian Conference of the Liquidators has invented a most unusual method. It is a simple and easy method. Listen to this:

"Having heard the communication of the Caucasian delegation to the effect that... it is necessary to demand national-cultural autonomy, this conference, while expressing no opinion on the merits of this demand, declares that such an interpretation of the clause of the programme which recognises the right of every nationality to self-determination does not contradict the precise meaning of the programme."

Thus, first of all they "express no opinion on the merits" of the question, and then they "declare." An original method....

And what does this original conference "declare"?

That the "demand" for national-cultural autonomy "does not contradict the precise meaning" of the programme, which recognises the right of nations to self determination.

Let us examine this proposition.

The clause on self-determination speaks of the rights of nations. According to this clause, nations have the right not only of autonomy but also of secession. It is a question of *political* self-determination. Whom did the Liquidators want to fool when they endeavoured to misinterpret this right of nations to political self-determination, which has long been recognised by the whole of international Social-Democracy?

Or perhaps the Liquidators will try to wriggle out of the situation and defend themselves by the sophism that cultural-national autonomy "does not contradict" the rights of nations? That is to say, if all the nations in a given state agree to arrange their affairs on the basis of cultural-national autonomy, they, the given sum of nations, are fully entitled to do so and nobody may *forcibly impose* a different form of political life on them. This is both new and clever. Should it not be added that, speaking generally, a nation has the right to abolish its own constitution, replace it by a system of tyranny and revert to the old order on the grounds that the nation, and the nation alone, has the right to determine its own destiny? We repeat: in this sense, neither cultural-national autonomy nor any other kind of nationalist reaction "contradicts" *the rights of nations*.

Is that what the esteemed conference wanted to say?

No, not that. It specifically says that cultural-national autonomy "does not contradict," not the rights of nations, but *"the precise meaning" of the programme*. The point here is the programme and not the rights of nations.

And that is quite understandable. If it were some nation that addressed itself to the conference of Liquidators, the conference might have directly declared that the nation has a right to cultural-national autonomy. But it was not a nation that addressed itself to the conference, but a "delegation" of Caucasian Social-Democrats – bad Social-Democrats, it is true, but Social Democrats nevertheless.

And they inquired not about the rights of nations, but whether cultural-national autonomy contradicted the *principles of Social-Democracy*, whether it did not "contradict" *"the precise meaning" of the programme of Social-Democracy.*

Thus, *the rights of nations and "the precise meaning" of the programme of Social-Democracy* are not one and the same thing.

Evidently, there are demands which, while they do not contradict the rights of nations, may yet contradict "the precise meaning" of the programme.

For example. The programme of the Social-Democrats contains a clause on freedom of religion. According to this clause any group of persons *have the right* to profess any religion they please: Catholicism, the religion of the Orthodox Church, etc. Social-Democrats will combat all forms of religious persecution, be it of members of the Orthodox Church, Catholics or Protestants. Does this mean that Catholicism, Protestantism, etc., "do not contradict the precise meaning" of the programme? No, it does not. Social-Democrats will always protest against persecution of Catholicism or Protestantism; they will always defend the right of nations to profess any religion they please; but at the same time, on the basis of a correct understanding of the interests of the proletariat, they will carry on agitation against Catholicism, Protestantism and the religion of the Orthodox Church in order to achieve the triumph of the socialist world outlook.

And they will do so just because there is no doubt that Protestantism, Catholicism, the religion of the Orthodox Church, etc., "contradict the precise meaning" of the programme, i.e., the correctly understood interests of the proletariat.

The same must be said of self-determination. Nations have a right to arrange their affairs as they please; they have a right to preserve any of their national institutions, whether beneficial or harmful – nobody can (nobody has a right to!) *forcibly* interfere in the life of a nation. But that does not mean that Social-Democracy will not combat and agitate against the harmful institutions of nations and against the inexpedient demands of nations. On the contrary, it is the duty of Social-Democracy to conduct such agitation and to endeavour to influence the will of nations so that the nations may arrange their affairs in the way that will best correspond to the interests of the proletariat. For this reason Social-Democracy, while fighting for the right of nations to self-determination, will at the same time agitate, for instance, against the secession of the Tatars, or against cultural-national autonomy for the Caucasian nations; for both, while not contradicting the *rights* of these nations, do contradict *"the precise meaning" of the programme*, i.e., the interests of the Caucasian proletariat.

Obviously, "the rights of nations" and the "precise meaning" of the programme are on two entirely different planes. Whereas the "precise meaning " of the programme expresses the interests of the proletariat, as scientifically formulated in the programme of the latter, the rights of nations may express the interests of any class – bourgeoisie, aristocracy, clergy, etc. – depending on the strength and influence of these classes. On the one hand are the *duties* of Marxists, on the other the *rights* of nations, which consist of various classes. The rights of nations and the principles of Social-Democracy may or may not "contradict" each other, just as, say, the pyramid of Cheops may or may not contradict the famous conference of the Liquidators. They are simply not comparable.

But it follows that the esteemed conference most unpardonably muddled two entirely different things. The result obtained was not a solution of the national question but an absurdity, according to which the rights of nations and the principles of Social-Democracy "do not contradict" each other, and, consequently, every demand of a nation may be made compatible with the interests of the proletariat; consequently, no demand of a nation which is striving for self-determination will "contradict the precise meaning" of the programme!

They pay no heed to logic....

It was this absurdity that gave rise to the now famous resolution of the conference of the Liquidators which declares that the demand for national-cultural autonomy "does not contradict the precise meaning" of the programme.

But it was not only the laws of logic that were violated by the conference of the Liquidators.

By sanctioning cultural-national autonomy it also violated its duty to Russian Social-Democracy. It most definitely did violate "the precise meaning" of the programme, for it is well known that the Second Congress, which adopted the programme, emphatically repudiated cultural-national autonomy. Here is what was said at the congress in this connection:

"*Goldblatt* (Bundist): ...I deem it necessary that special institutions be set up to protect the freedom of cultural development of nationalities, and I therefore propose that the following words be added to § 8: '*and the creation of institutions which will guarantee them complete freedom of cultural development'.*" (This, as we know, is the Bund's definition of cultural-national autonomy. – *J. St.*)

"*Martynov* pointed out that general institutions must be so constituted as to protect particular interests also. It is impossible to create a *special* institution to guarantee freedom for cultural development of the nationalities.

"*Yegorov*: On the question of nationality we can adopt only negative proposals, i.e., we are opposed to all restrictions upon nationality. But we, as Social-Democrats, are not concerned with whether any particular nationality will develop as such. That is a spontaneous process.

"*Koltsov*: The delegates from the Bund are always offended when their nationalism is referred to. Yet the amendment proposed by the delegate from the Bund is of a purely nationalist character. We are asked to take purely offensive measures in order to support even nationalities that are dying out."

In the end "*Goldblatt's amendment was rejected by the majority, only three votes being cast for it.*"

Thus it is clear that the conference of the Liquidators did "contradict the precise meaning" of the programme. It violated the programme.

The Liquidators are now trying to justify themselves by referring to the Stockholm Congress, which they allege sanctioned cultural-national autonomy. Thus, V. Kossovsky writes:

"As we know, according to the agreement adopted by the Stockholm Congress, the Bund was allowed to preserve its national programme (pending a decision on the national question by a general Party congress). This congress recorded that national-cultural autonomy at any rate does not contradict the general Party programme."[*]

But the efforts of the Liquidators are in vain. The Stockholm Congress never thought of sanctioning the programme of the Bund – it merely agreed to leave the question open for the time being. The

---

[*] *Nasha Zarya*, No. 9-10, 1912, p. 120.

brave Kossovsky did not have enough courage to tell the whole truth. But the facts speak for themselves. Here they are:

"An amendment was moved by Galin: 'The question of the national programme *is left open in view of the fact that it is not being examined* by the congress.' (*For* – 50 votes, *against* – 32.)

"*Voice*: What does that mean – open?

"*Chairman*: When we say that the national question is left open, it means that the Bund may maintain its decision on this question until the next congress"[*] (our italics – *J. St.*).

As you see, the congress even did "not examine" the question of the national programme of the Bund – it simply left it "open," leaving the Bund itself to decide the fate of its programme until the next general congress met. In other words, the Stockholm Congress avoided the question, expressing no opinion on cultural-national autonomy one way or another. The conference of the Liquidators, however, most definitely undertakes to give an opinion on the matter, declares cultural-national autonomy to be acceptable, and endorses it in the name of the Party programme.

The difference is only too evident.

Thus, in spite of all its artifices, the conference of the Liquidators did not advance the national question a single step.

All it could do was to squirm before the Bund and the Caucasian national-Liquidators.

VII

THE NATIONAL QUESTION IN RUSSIA

It remains for us to suggest a positive solution of the national question.

We take as our starting point that the question can be solved only in intimate connection with the present situation in Russia.

Russia is in a transitional period, when "normal," "constitutional" life has not yet been established and when the political crisis has not yet been settled. Days of storm and "complications" are ahead. And this gives rise to the movement, the present and the future movement, the aim of which is to achieve complete democratisation.

---

[*] See *Nashe Slovo*, No. 8, 1906, p. 53.

It is in connection with this movement that the national question must be examined.

Thus the complete democratisation of the country is the basis and condition for the solution of the national question.

When seeking a solution of the question we must take into account not only the situation at home but also the situation abroad. Russia is situated between Europe and Asia, between Austria and China. The growth of democracy in Asia is inevitable. The growth of imperialism in Europe is not fortuitous. In Europe, capital is beginning to feel cramped, and it is reaching out towards foreign countries in search of new markets, cheap labour and new fields of investment. But this leads to external complications and to war. No one can assert that the Balkan War[14] is the end and not the beginning of the complications. It is quite possible, therefore, that a combination of internal and external conditions may arise in which one or another nationality in Russia may find it necessary to raise and settle the question of its independence. And, of course, it is not for Marxists to create obstacles in such cases.

But it follows that Russian Marxists cannot dispense with the right of nations to self-determination.

Thus, *the right of self-determination is an essential element* in the solution of the national question.

Further. What must be our attitude towards nations which for one reason or another will prefer to remain within the framework of the whole?

We have seen that cultural-national autonomy is unsuitable. Firstly, it is artificial and impracticable, for it proposes artificially to draw into a single nation people whom the march of events, real events, is disuniting and dispersing to every corner of the country. Secondly, it stimulates nationalism, because it leads to the viewpoint in favour of the "demarcation" of people according to national *curiae*, the "organisation" of nations, the "preservation" and cultivation of "national peculiarities" – all of which are entirely incompatible with Social-Democracy. It is not fortuitous that the Moravian separatists in the Reichsrat, having severed themselves from the German Social-Democratic deputies, have united with the Moravian bourgeois deputies to form a single, so to speak, Moravian "kolo." Nor is it fortuitous that the separatists of the Bund have got themselves involved in nationalism by acclaiming the "Sabbath" and "Yiddish." There are no Bundist deputies yet in the Duma, but in the Bund area there is a clerical-reactionary Jewish community, in the "controlling institutions" of which the Bund is arranging, for a beginning, a "get-together" of the Jewish workers and bourgeois.[*] Such is the logic of cultural-national autonomy.

Thus, *national* autonomy does not solve the problem.

What, then, is the way out?

The only correct solution is *regional* autonomy, autonomy for such crystallised units as Poland, Lithuania, the Ukraine, the Caucasus, etc.

The advantage of regional autonomy consists, first of all, in the fact that it does not deal with a fiction bereft of territory, but with a definite population inhabiting a definite territory. Next, it does not divide people according to nations, it does not strengthen national barriers; on the contrary, it breaks down these barriers and unites the population in such a manner as to open the way for division of a different kind, division according to classes. Finally, it makes it possible to utilise the natural wealth of the region and to develop its productive forces in the best possible way without awaiting the decisions of a common centre – functions which are not inherent features of cultural-national autonomy.

Thus, *regional autonomy is an essential element* in the solution of the national question.

Of course, not one of the regions constitutes a compact, homogeneous nation, for each is interspersed with national minorities. Such are the Jews in Poland, the Letts in Lithuania, the Russians in the Caucasus, the Poles in the Ukraine, and so on. It may be feared, therefore, that the minorities will be oppressed by the national majorities. But there will be grounds for fear only if the old order continues to prevail in the country. Give the country complete democracy and all grounds for fear will vanish.

It is proposed to bind the dispersed minorities into a single national union. But what the minorities want is not an artificial union, but real rights in the localities they inhabit. What can such a union give them *without* complete democratisation? On the other hand, what need is there for a national union *when there* is complete democratisation?

What is it that particularly agitates a national minority?

---

[*] See *Report of the Eighth Conference of the Bund*, the concluding part of the resolution on the community.

A minority is discontented not because there is no national union but because it does not enjoy the right to use its native language. Permit it to use its native language and the discontent will pass of itself.

A minority is discontented not because there is no artificial union but because it does not possess its own schools. Give it its own schools and all grounds for discontent will disappear.

A minority is discontented not because there is no national union, but because it does not enjoy liberty of conscience (religious liberty), liberty of movement, etc. Give it these liberties and it will cease to be discontented.

Thus, *equal rights of nations in all forms* (*language, schools, etc.*) *is an essential element* in the solution of the national question. Consequently, a state law based on complete democratisation of the country is required, prohibiting all national privileges without exception and every kind of disability or restriction on the rights of national minorities.

That, and that alone, is the real, not a paper guarantee of the rights of a minority.

One may or may not dispute the existence of a logical connection between organisational federalism and cultural-national autonomy. But one cannot dispute the fact that the latter creates an atmosphere favouring unlimited federalism, developing into complete rupture, into separatism. If the Czechs in Austria and the Bundists in Russia began with autonomy, passed to federation and ended in separatism, there can be no doubt that an important part in this was played by the nationalist atmosphere that is naturally generated by cultural-national autonomy. It is not fortuitous that national autonomy and organisational federalism go hand in hand. It is quite understandable. Both demand demarcation according to nationalities. Both presume organisation according to nationalities. The similarity is beyond question. The only difference is that in one case the population as a whole is divided, while in the other it is the Social-Democratic workers who are divided.

We know where the demarcation of workers according to nationalities leads to. The disintegration of a united workers' party, the splitting of trade unions according to nationalities, aggravation of national friction, national strike-breaking, complete demoralisation within the ranks of Social-Democracy – such are the results of organisational federalism. This is eloquently borne out by the history of Social-Democracy in Austria and the activities of the Bund in Russia.

The only cure for this is organisation on the basis of internationalism.

To unite locally the workers of all nationalities of Russia into *single, integral* collective bodies, to unite these collective bodies into a *single* party – such is the task.

It goes without saying that a party structure of this kind does not preclude, but on the contrary presumes, wide autonomy for the *regions* within the single integral party.

The experience of the Caucasus proves the expediency of this type of organisation. If the Caucasians have succeeded in overcoming the national friction between the Armenian and Tatar workers; if they have succeeded in safeguarding the population against the possibility of massacres and shooting affrays; if in Baku, that kaleidoscope of national groups, national conflicts are now no longer possible, and if it has been possible to draw the workers there into the single current of a powerful movement, then the international structure of the Caucasian Social-Democracy was not the least factor in bringing this about.

The type of organisation influences not only practical work. It stamps an indelible impression the whole mental life of the worker. The worker lives the life of his organisation, which stimulates his intellectual growth and educates him. And thus, acting within his organisation and continually meeting there comrades from other nationalities, and side by side with them waging a common struggle under the leadership of a common collective body, he becomes deeply imbued with the idea that workers are *primarily* members of one class family, members of the united army of socialism. And this cannot but have a tremendous educational value for large sections of the working class.

Therefore, the international type of organisation serves as a school of fraternal sentiments and is a tremendous agitational factor on behalf of internationalism.

But this is not the case with an organisation on the basis of nationalities. When the workers are organised according to nationality they isolate themselves within their national shells, fenced off from each other by organisational barriers. The stress is laid not on what is *common* to the workers but on what distinguishes them from each other. In this type of organisation the worker is *primarily* a member of his nation: a Jew, a Pole, and so on. It is not surprising that *national* federalism in organisation inculcates in the workers a spirit of national seclusion.

Therefore, the national type of organisation is a school of national narrow-mindedness and stagnation.

Thus we are confronted by two *fundamentally* different types of organisation: the type based on international solidarity and the type based on the organisational "demarcation" of the workers according to nationalities.

Attempts to reconcile these two types have so far been vain. The compromise rules of the Austrian Social-Democratic Party drawn up in Wimberg in 1897 were left hanging in the air. The Austrian party fell to pieces and dragged the trade unions with it. "Compromise" proved to be not only utopian, but harmful. Strasser is right when he says that "separatism achieved its first triumph at the Wimberg Party Congress."* The same is true in Russia. The "compromise" with the federalism of the Bund which took place at the Stockholm Congress ended in a complete fiasco. The Bund violated the Stockholm compromise. Ever since the Stockholm Congress the Bund has been an obstacle in the way of union of the workers locally in a *single* organisation, which would include workers of all nationalities. And the Bund has obstinately persisted in its separatist tactics in spite of the fact that in 1907 and in 1908 Russian Social-Democracy repeatedly demanded that unity should at last be established from below among the workers of all nationalities.[15] The Bund, which began with organisational national autonomy, in fact passed to federalism, only to end in complete rupture, separatism. And by breaking with the Russian Social-Democratic Party it caused disharmony and disorganisation in the ranks of the latter. Let us recall the Jagiello affair,[16] for instance.

The path of "compromise" must therefore be discarded as utopian and harmful.

One thing or the other: *either* the federalism of the Bund, in which case the Russian Social-Democratic Party must reform itself on a basis of "demarcation" of the workers according to nationalities; or an international type of organisation, in which case the Bund must reform itself on a basis of territorial autonomy after the pattern of the Caucasian, Lettish and Polish Social-Democracies, and thus

---

* See his *Der Arbeiter und die Nation*, 1912.

make possible the direct union of the Jewish workers with the workers of the other nationalities of Russia.

There is no middle course: principles triumph, they do not "compromise."

Thus, *the principle of international solidarity of the workers is an essential element* in the solution of the national question.

Vienna, January 1913

First published in *Prosveshcheniye*,[17]

Nos. 3-5, March-May 1913

Signed: *K. Stalin*

NOTES

[1] *Marxism and the National Question* was written at the end of 1912 and the beginning of 1913 in Vienna. It first appeared in the magazine *Prosveshcheniye (Enlightenment)*, Nos. 3-5, 1913, under the title "The National Question and Social-Democracy" and was signed K. Stalin. In 1914 it was published by the Priboy Publishers, St. Petersburg, as a separate pamphlet entitled *The National Question and Marxism*. By order of the Minister of the Interior the pamphlet was withdrawn from all public libraries and reading rooms. In 1920 the article was republished by the People's Commissariat for Nationalities in a *Collection of Articles* by J. V. Stalin on the national question (State Publishing House, Tula). In 1934 the article was included in the book: J. Stalin, *Marxism and the National and Colonial Question. A Collection of Articles and Speeches.* Lenin, in his article "The National Programme of the R.S.D.L.P.," referring to the reasons which were lending prominence to the national question at that period, wrote: "This state of affairs, and the principles of the national programme of Social-Democracy, have already been dealt with recently in theoretical Marxist literature (prime place must here be given to Stalin's article)." In February 1913, Lenin wrote to Maxim Gorky: "We have a wonderful Georgian here who has sat down to write a big article for *Prosveshcheniye* after collecting *all* the Austrian and other material." Learning that it was proposed to print the article with the reservation that it was for discussion only, Lenin vigorously objected, and wrote: "Of course, we are absolutely against this. It is a *very good* article. The question is a burning issue, and we shall not yield one jot of principle to the Bundist scum." (Archives of the Marx-Engels-Lenin Institute.) Soon after J. V. Stalin's arrest, in March 1913, Lenin wrote to the editors of *Sotsial-Demokrat*: "...Arrests among us are very heavy. Koba has been taken.... Koba managed to write a long article (for three issues of *Prosveshcheniye*) on the national question. Good! We must fight for the truth and against separatists and opportunists of the Bund and among the Liquidators." (Archives of the Marx-Engels-Lenin Institute.)

[2] Zionism – a reactionary nationalist trend of the Jewish bourgeoisie, which had followers among the intellectuals and the more backward sections of the Jewish workers. The Zionists endeavoured to isolate the Jewish working-class masses from the general struggle of the proletariat. Today the Zionist organisations are the agents of the American imperialists in their machinations directed against the U.S.S.R. and the People's Democracies and the revolutionary movement in capitalist and colonial countries.

[3] The Brünn Parteitag, or Congress, of the Austrian Social-Democratic Party was held on September 24-29, 1899. The resolution on the national question adopted by this congress is quoted by J. V. Stalin in the next chapter of this work (see p. 28).

[4] "Thank God we have no parliament here" – the words uttered by V. Kokovtsev, tsarist Minister of Finance (later Prime Minister), in the State Duma on April 24, 1908.

[5] See Chapter II of the *Manifesto of the Communist Party* by Karl Marx and Frederick Engels (Karl Marx and Frederick Engels, *Selected Works*, Eng. ed., Vol. I, Moscow 1951, p. 49).

[6] The Vienna Congress (or *Wimberg* Congress – after the name of the hotel in which it met) of the Austrian Social-Democratic Party was held June 6-12, 1897.

[7] The reference is to an article by Karl Marx entitled "Zur Judenfrage" ("The Jewish Question"), published in 1844 in the *Deutsch-Französische Jahrbücher*. (See Marx/Engels, *Gesamtausgabe*, Erste Abteilung, Band 1, Halbband 1.)

[8] The Eighth Conference of the Bund was held in September 1910 in Lvov.

[9] In an article entitled "Another Splitters' Conference," published in the newspaper *Za Partiyu*, October 2 (15), 1912, G. V. Plekhanov condemned the "August" Conference of the Liquidators and described the stand of the Bundists and Caucasian Social-Democrats as an adaptation of socialism to nationalism. Kossovsky, leader of the Bundists, criticised Plekhanov in a letter to the Liquidators' magazine *Nasha Zarya*.

[10] The Seventh Congress of the Bund was held in Lvov at the end of August and beginning of September 1906.

[11] *Iskra* (*The Spark*) – the first all-Russian illegal Marxist newspaper founded by V. I. Lenin in 1900 (see J. V. Stalin, *Works*, Vol. 1, p. 400, Note 26).

[12] *Karl Vanêk* – a Czech Social-Democrat who took an openly chauvinist and separatist stand.

[13] *Chveni Tskhoveba* (*Our Life*) – a daily newspaper published by the Georgian Mensheviks in Kutais from July 1 to 22, 1912.

[14] The reference is to the first Balkan War, which broke out in October 1912 between Bulgaria, Serbia, Greece and Montenegro on the one hand, and Turkey on the other.

[15] See the resolutions of the Fourth (the "Third All-Russian") Conference of the R.S.D.L.P. held November 5-12, 1907, and of the Fifth (the "All-Russian 1908") Conference of the R.S.D.L.P. held December 21-27, 1908 (January 3-9, 1909) (see *Resolutions and Deci-*

sions of C.P.S.U. (B.) Congresses, Conferences and Central Committee Plenums, Vol. 1, 6th Russ. ed., 1940, pp. 118, 131).

[16] E. J. Jagiello – a member of the Polish Socialist Party (P.P.S.), was elected to the Fourth State Duma for Warsaw as a result of a bloc formed by the Bund, the Polish Socialist Party and the bourgeois nationalists against the Polish Social-Democrats. By a vote of the seven Menshevik Liquidators against the six Bolsheviks, the Social-Democratic group in the Duma adopted a resolution that Jagiello be accepted as a member of the group.

[17] *Prosveshcheniye (Enlightenment)* – a Bolshevik monthly published legally in St. Petersburg, the first issue appearing in December 1911. It was directed by Lenin through regular correspondence with the members of the editorial board in Russia (M. A. Savelyev, M. S. Olminsky, A. I. Elizarova). When J. V. Stalin was in St. Petersburg he took an active part in the work of the journal. *Prosveshcheniye* was closely connected with *Pravda*. In June 1914, on the eve of the First World War, it was suppressed by the government. One double number appeared in the autumn of 1917.

Made in the USA
Middletown, DE
20 December 2015